DEFINING
MOMENTS
IN
HISTORY

DEFINING MOMENTS IN HISTORY

Published by TAJ BOOKS 2003
27 Ferndown Gardens
Cobham
Surrey
KT11 2BH
UK
www.tajbooks.com

Design and layout Copyright © TAJ Books Ltd

Picture Research Veronica Jaitly
Design Scott Gibson
Text and Editorial Forty Editorial Services Ltd

ISBN 1-84406-016-0

Printed in China.
1 2 3 4 5 06 05 04 03

Captions for photos in Introduction:
Page 6
The Berlin Wall is pulled down.

Page 7
P-192 Smoke rises from the eruption of Mt. Oyama August 2000.

Page 8
The Russian Mir space station seen from US space shuttle *Atlantis*, January 16, 1997.

Page 9
9-11: the World Trade Center after the towers collapsed.

CONTENTS

This book is about the people, events, discoveries, and disasters that changed the world forever. They pinpoint a moment in time when nothing could ever be the same again. The classic question for the last fifty years was "where were you when Kennedy was shot?" Now, tragically, it has changed to "what were you doing when you heard about the World Trade Center?" Both events crystallized a moment in time before which the world was a simpler, safer, place.

Ironically, both good news and bad can bring people together and instil a unity of purpose previously lacking. Perhaps, nowhere is this better illustrated than in the events following the outrage of 9/11. The people of the United States of America buried their differences in the fight against the common enemy, and New York, that most diverse city, found a togetherness and unity it had never experienced before.

Not all world-changing events are so obviously shattering or have occurred in the public eye: the discovery of the double helix structure of DNA by James Watson and Francis Crick (with the help of Rosalind Franklin) which decoded human genetics quietly took place in a laboratory in Cambridge, England in 1953. Similarly ground-breaking were the remarkable and top secret experiments conducted by J. Robert Oppenheimer and his team who built the first atom bomb at Los Alamos in 1943. This nuclear research led directly to the dropping of the atomic bomb on Hiroshima (August 6, 1946) and then on Nagasaki three days later. The end of the war in the Pacific on August 14, only a few days later, was a direct result of the massive loss of life occasioned by these explosions. It undoubtedly saved the Allies from the enormous casualties that would have been sustained during an amphibious assault on Japan. From that time onward, the nuclear threat became a potent deterrent. Nation

states became divided into those who had the "bomb" and those who didn't.

The starting and ending of wars are major defining moments, both in the lives of the individuals involved, as well as for the world in general. The twentieth century was scarred by two global wars, as well as many other dreadful conflagrations that took a heavy toll in both military and civilian lives. Such wars alter the course of history as well as political boundaries. As a by-product, war is also a time of great technological change as governments and organizations pour money into research in an attempt to get ahead of the opposition. The prime example of this is the investigation and development of rocket technology: all the major protagonists in the Second World War were desperately researching rocket power because the accurate and powerful delivery of ordnance into the battlefield or other targets could be decisive to the outcome of the conflict. After the war German rocket technicians

were spirited out of Germany and into U.S. and British laboratories, most notably the German genius Wernher von Braun who was at the heart of the Mercury rocket program and, ultimately, played a large part in getting man onto the surface of the Moon.

The space race opened the world's eyes to the heavens and the stars beyond. Spacemen became heroes. The Soviet cosmonaut Yuri Gagarin, was the first man in space and instantly became a celebrity around the world. His colleague, Valentina Tereshkova, was the first woman to achieve this feat. The first American in space was Alan Shepard on May 5, 1961. It is remarkable to think that it took less than a decade between these first brief moments in space and the American astronaut Neil Armstrong (1930–) walking on the Moon. On that July day in 1969 science fiction became fact; the first small step was taken in a voyage of discovery away from our own world. We can now send rockets and

probes out into deepest space and no one knows what they will encounter, space is the newest frontier. Our next advances could be literally beyond our imagination. More than this, when President Kennedy looked up to the sky and announced that man would step on the Moon, it was the signal that humans were bold enough and brave enough as well as clever enough to leave the confines of Mother Earth.

Space is still the greatest challenge mankind faces, but in the years since the lunar landings there has been a strong urge to improve the lot of those at home. Scientific developments in the twentieth century have gone a long way toward solving many of the world's problems. Some of the most important changes on a day-to-day basis have been in the realm of transport. At the beginning of the century there was little by way of personal transport—most people had to use trains, horses, or their own feet. Travelling any distance was a rare event and a form of

endurance rather than a luxury. Then the development of the internal combustion engine and the Model T Ford enabled individual freedom of movement to a level undreamt of before. The internal combustion engine has been under constant development and new models of improved engine and vehicle appear every year. In the developed world almost every adult owns or has access to a motor vehicle of some sort. Millions of cars fill our roads and their need for fuel has made the petrochemical industry one of the most powerful factions in global politics.

An even more amazing development in the early twentieth century was that of flight. Orville and Frank Wright first took to the air in their own machine on December 17, 1903, at Kittyhawk, North Carolina and others quickly followed. At last mankind's great dream of joining the birds in the sky became reality. As the century progressed the jet engine was developed by Frank Whittle and the first successful flight was by a Gloster

aircraft in May 1941. Since then aero engines have been improved and the earth has shrunk as a result. Cheap air travel became possible for everyone—and so another industry grew: the travel business, devised to allow holidaymakers to use such an easy form of travel.

But technology has its downside. In 1979 the U.S. suffered its worst nuclear accident at Three Mile Island when the nuclear reactor at Harrisburg, Pennsylvania, went into meltdown causing widespread panic and dismay. The massive toxic spill of the oil container ships *Amoco Cadiz* (March 1977) and *Exxon Valdez* (March 1989) to name but two, were ecological disasters on a massive scale, and the dreadful catastrophes of the nuclear powerplant leak at Chernobyl (April 26, 1986) and the toxic gas cloud at Bhophal (December 3, 1984) in India showed just how dangerous and unstable modern technologies can be.

Advances in transportation have also cast their shadow. The most famous are the dreadful losses of life caused by sinking ships or crashing aircraft—such as the *Titanic* (April 14, 1912) or *Luisitania* (May 7, 1915), and the catastrophic *Hindenburg* airship fire (May 6, 1937) or the carnage at Tenerife (March 27, 1977). Not all devastating accidents carry a huge death toll but are nevertheless significant— for example the shocking explosion of the space shuttle, *Challenger*, (January 31, 1986) and the death of her crew of seven in front of the watching world, or the dreadful railroad crash at Paddington (October 5, 1999) which killed 31 and injured more, and left many Britons nervous of rail travel. All these dreadful disasters and many more bring home the sobering price of advancement.

Not all catastrophes are caused by technology; natural disasters have caused even greater death tolls. The century had only just got going in 1902 when Mount Pelée exploded on the small Caribbean island of Martinique. Everyone in the town of Saint Pierre died when the dormant volcano exploded except one criminal in an underground cell. Just four years later the San Andreas fault split resulting in a massive earthquake which struck San Francisco (April 18, 1906) leaving the city a mass of rubble. Such earthquakes happen regularly but rarely in such populous areas, although recent quakes in Sichuan, China (May 11, 1974) left an estimated 20,000 dead and the earthquake under Kobe, Japan (1995) left 5,000 dead. Other disastrous natural phenomena occur on a regular basis but their scale is such that little can be done to prevent disaster; two such examples are the regular floods in Bangladesh and annual hurricanes in the Caribbean, both of which have accounted for thousands dead and missing as well as devastated homes and livings.

Whether caused by man or nature, famine is the silent killer accountable for

millions of innocent lives. Nobody knows how many died in the famines in the Soviet Union in the 1930s, or in Biafra following the dreadful civil war in Nigeria in the 1960s, or on the hot, dusty, Somali peninsula in the 1980s and 1990s. The death toll from twentieth century famines alone number many millions.

It is human nature to dwell on the disasters that afflicted the world: the positives, however, abound. In spite of all the disasters, general health levels improved and the average lifespan increased. Gigantic leaps in hygiene and nutrition as well as advances in medicine, have all but eradicated a number of global illnesses and improved the lot of many on earth. There are fewer totalitarian states, and the improvement in global communications has done much to ensure that light is shone into dark corners, and that tyrants such as Saddam Hussein will be punished.

An interesting barometer of the modern world is the sports industry. A world that

has time to play and watch sports is one that must be becoming healthier—even though evil concerns have tried to hijack the big events for their own good—one thinks of the Nazis' Olympics in 1936, the Communist version in 1980, and the terrorism of Munich. Nevertheless, sports have become more important in most peoples' lives since the advent of television.

Sportspeople have always been heroes but now the viewer can feel an intimate involvement and the big sporting occasions such as the Superbowl, Ryder Cup, or the soccer World Cup are guaranteed to attract millions of viewers.

Jesse Owens became a hero many years after his courageous and triumphant achievements—four gold medals—at the Berlin Olympics in 1936 because his exploits were only reported in newspapers and on radio. It took television to turn the sportsmen and women into superstars. One of the first and one of the greatest was Mohammed Ali whose fights were

enthusiastically followed by millions all around the world.

Sport is the competitive end of the entertainment industry which is itself a multibillion dollar business, and the people who control it are among the most powerful in the world. The entertainers, whether musicians or actors, are the public face of the industry and they have gained a significance completely out of proportion to their talent. Film and TV stars are recognized globally and their exploits are followed by a multi-cultural audience.

It may be difficult to support the argument that in the defining moments of the modern age sports or entertainment weigh as heavily as science or medical advances, but to the average person they often feel as if they do—particularly if their team won!

This book shows the range of mankind's achievement and the staggering ability of our species to create, develop, adapt, inspire, and imagine a better future.

1900
Marie and Pierre Curie discover and isolate radium.

1901
Nobel prizes—for physics, chemistry, physiology or medicine, literature, and peace—first awarded.

1905
Albert Einstein's theory of relativity published (and a further paper in 1916).

1909
Tschaikovsky's *Nutcracker Suite* is recorded and packaged—the first album.

1912
Motorized movie cameras replace hand cranks.

1920
In England, Guglielmo Marconi creates the first short wave radio connection.and establishes a worldwide radio telegraph network.

1921
Insulin isolated by Charles Best and Frederick Banting.

1924
Insecticides are used for the first time on crops.

1925
Edwin Hubble announces his discovery of the expansion of the universe.

1926
John Logie Baird gives first demonstration of a television image.

1928
Alexander Fleming discovers penicillin but has to wait 11 years until the drug can be produced.

1932
John Cockroft and Ernest Walton split a lithium nucleus with the first successful use of a particle accelerator.

1935
Sir Robert Watson-Watt originates plan for radio pulse-echo detection of aircraft leading to radar stations.

1936
Single-lens reflex (SLR) camera developed in Germany. Alan Turing publishes theory of computability that will lead to the production of computers.

1937
George Stibitz of Bell Labs invents the electrical digital calculator.

1945
First atomic explosions—at Alamogordo on July 16, Hiroshima (August 6), and Nagasaki (August 9).

1949
Whirlwind at MIT is the first real time computer.

1951
H-Bomb developed, primarily by Edward Teller at Los Alamos. First successful test at Eniwetok Atoll, 1952.

1952
Jonas E. Salk develops the first polio vaccine.

1956
The first transatlantic telephone cable between Britain and North America begins operation.
The first hard disk drive is created at IBM.

1957
Sputnik 1, first artificial satellite, is launched by the USSR. US Explorer 1 launched four months later.

1960
US TIROS 1, worlds first weather satellite, is launched. Introduction of the Contraceptive Pill.
Laser developed in US laboratories.

1963
Instamatic cameras with drop-in cartridges; more than 50 million will be sold.
Maarten Schmidt discovers Quasars.

1964
A local area network (LAN) is created for atomic weapons research.
First version of Moore's Law: Microprocessor speed will double each year.

1967
First Heart Transplant by Dr Christiaan Barnard. The first floppy disk is produced by IBM. Prerecorded movies on videotape sold for home television sets.

The story of scientific development almost defines the twentieth century. These were the single most important years for science in the entire history of mankind. Scientists had been developing momentum since the Italian Renaissance but it was the twentieth century when science exploded and previously only dreamed of achievements became possible. Mankind can at last travel distance at speed, he can fly and reach the stars. He can have his own personal motor car and drive through lit streets, one person can talk to another on the other side of the world, pictures can move, and extensive calculations and problems can be solved with a few keystrokes on a computer—and all this is just the tip of the iceberg.

In the field of medicine amazing achievements have been made in the 20th century. The first breakthrough occurred in 1900 when Marie Curie discovered radium and x-radiography which in turn led to the development of x-rays and methods of diagnosing physical internal problems without cutting the patient open first. In 1921 the hormone insulin was discovered by Charles Best and Frederick Bantin, this is still used as the main treatment for diabetes. Another important advance was Alexander Fleming's discovery of the bacterial antibiotic penicillin in 1928.

In much of the world childbirth and infant mortality are no longer the greatly feared regular killers they once were. Many childhood diseases, such as polio, have been virtually eradicated thanks to the work of people such as Jonas Salk who developed the first polio vaccine in 1952. The technology to transplant entire organs has been developed—the work pioneered by Dr Christiaan Barnard who caused a worldwide sensation when he performed the first successful human heart transplant at Groot Schuur Hospital, Cape Town in December 1967. His first patient, Louis Washkansky survived for 18 days before dying of pneumonia, but the next, Philip Blaiberg, lived for almost two years. Today, organ transplants, while not commonplace, are a regular part of hospital surgery.

SCIENCE

At the end of the century, on June 26, 2000, the human genome was deciphered which meant that the totality of the DNA sequence—30,000 genes—has been revealed. This shows the sequences of the three billion chemical base pairs that make up human DNA. Among many other things this will help in the diagnosis of disease and help earlier detection of genetic disorder. This breakthrough technology is confidently expected to revolutionize medicine as it will also enable laboratories to tailor drugs for specific problems.

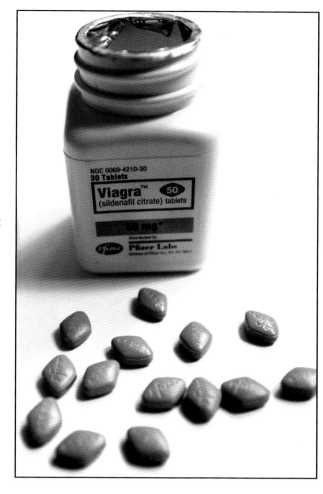

No study of the 20th century would be complete without acknowledgment of the computer revolution. Scientists have long dreamt of a machine that could calculate and break down, analyse, and order information. The first pioneering steps were taken by Charles Babbage (1791–1871) but technology had to catch up with human imagination and this did not happen until the 20th century. World War II codebreakers helped to develop the technology as did companies like IBM. But it needed the birth of the microprocessor in 1971 to reduce the size of computers to a more manageable and economic desktop machine.

In 1975 IBM produced the first personal computer, it weighed 50lb and cost $9,000 for 16k, or $20,000 for a 64k machine. In 1981 IBM launched the PC, the personal computer and as the cost came down more people were able to buy one to use at home.

Technology improved fast and in 1984 the Apple Macintosh was introduced. The industry was highly lucrative and attracted some of the brightest minds on the planet, including Bill Gates the inspiration behind Microsoft whose first Windows 1.0 operating system was shipped in 1985.

Simultaneously with the PC the Internet was being developed and within a few short years the Net was a phenomenon available to everyone who had access to a computer and modem. Computers have got faster, smaller, lighter, and more powerful. Laptop computers, once prohibitively expensive, are now commonplace. The computer has become indispensable to everyday life and is used as a prime work tool by millions of people every day.

1968
Intelsat III completes global communications satellite loop.
An Intel 1 KB RAM microchip reaches the market.
Canadian filmmakers invent giant IMAX large screen movie projection system using 70mm film.

1969
Audio music tapes sold with Dolby Noise Reduction.
Kenneth Thompson creates the Unix Operating System for computers.
UCLA computer sends data to a computer at Stanford, foreshadowing the Internet.

1970
Corning Glass Works spins out optical fiber clear enough for light pulses.
Barcodes on products supply pricing and stock data.

1971
Birth of the Microprocessor allowed the development of small desktop computers.
The first traffic in Email.
Intel builds the 4004 microprocessor, "a computer on a chip."
Cellphone invented, giving unlimited communication.

1973
Xerox sets up a LAN (local area network) called Ethernet.

1975
IBM portable computer, 50 lb., cost $9,000 for 16K, $20,000 for 64K machines.

1976
Sony's Betamax and JVC's VHS battle for lucrative home market—Sony looses out within a few years.

1978
Louise Brown, the world's first test tube baby.
Konica of Japan, manufacture the point-and-shoot, autofocus camera.

1981
The PC (personal computer) is launched by IBM.
From Microsoft, the MSDOS 1.0 operating system.

1982
Sony of Japan and Philips of the Netherlands bring out the compact disc.

1983
Internet domains get easy to remember names instead of strings of numbers.

1984
Apple Macintosh and IBM PC AT are introduced.

1985
Microsoft ships the Windows 1.0 operating system.

1986
Sony revolutionize computer gaming with the Game Boy, 8-bit operating system.

1987
Prozac, the happiness drug gets ok from the FDA.
Excel, PageMaker are born.

1991
The world wide web appears—an instant sensation.

1993
Nokia sends text messages between mobile phones

1994
The Yahoo search engine is started by two Stanford graduate engineering students.
Amazon.com starts selling books online, will become the Web's hottest retailer.

1996
From Microsoft: Hotmail.com, a Web-based email site.

1997
The first clone: Dolly the sheep is born.
DVDs go on sale revolutionizing home entertainment.

1998
Viagra, anti-impotence drug gets FDA Approval.
Traffic on the Internet, network of networks, is doubling every 100 days.

1999
The Ikonos satellite can detect an object on Earth as small as a card table.

The 30,000 gene sequence of the human genome deciphered; will revolutionize medicine.

2001
US authorizes stem cell research.

Above: Professor Albert Einstein (1879–1955) in 1920. Einstein's general theories of relativity (1905 and 1916) won him a Nobel Prize for Physics in 1921. His name is mentioned in the same breath as Newton and Galileo as one of the greatest scientists to have lived.

Above Right: Photograph taken around August 1926 of John Logie Baird (1888–1946), the television pioneer, with his first TV apparatus which he presented to the London Science Museum.

Above Left: Madame Marie Curie (1867–1934), discoverer of radium and X-rays. Said to have invented the term "radioactivity," Marie and husband Pierre jointly won the 1903 Nobel Prize for Physics. She would win a second Nobel in 1911, this time for chemistry, for isolating pure radium. She died of leukemia, probably as a result of her experimentation.

Left: A cheerful greeting from Professor Charles Best (1899–1978), at age 72, and his wife Margaret, pictured at Heathrow Airport, London, on their arrival from Toronto. Canadians Charles Best (then a research student) and Frederick Banting isolated the hormone insulin in 1921. Banting shared his 1923 Nobel for medicine with Best who would go on to become one of the most successful of medical scientists.

Right: Sir Alexander Fleming, here at age 73, was a Scottish bacteriologist who discovered Penicillin in 1928. Knighted in 1944, he is seen with his wife, Lady Fleming.

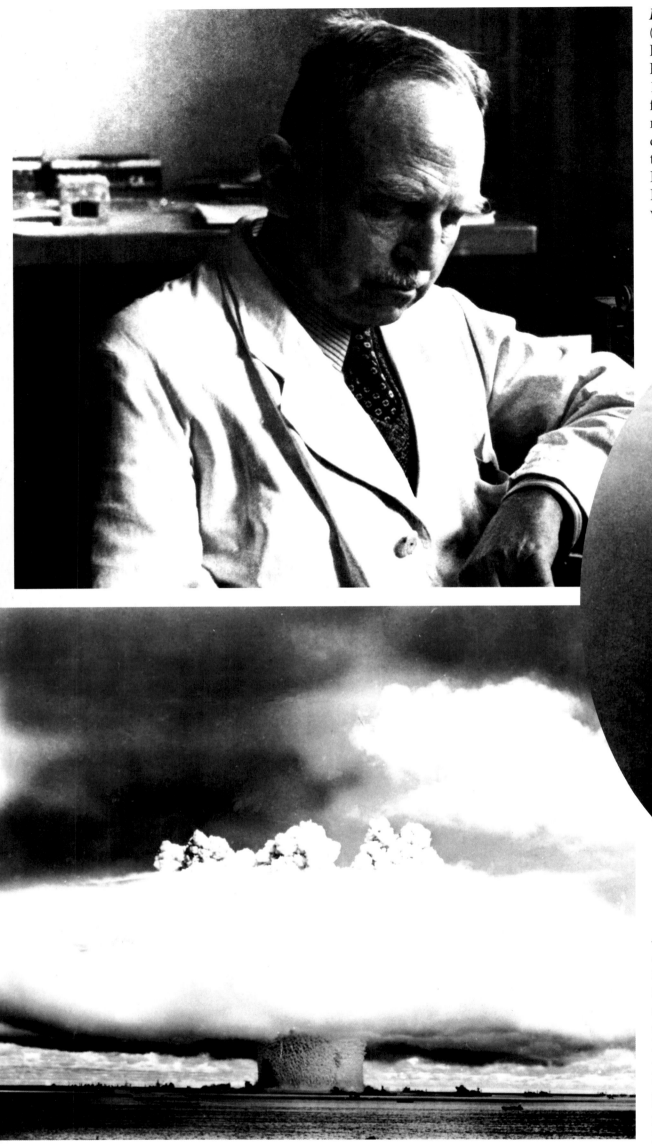

Left: German chemist Otto Hahn (1879–1968) worked with Rutherford and Fischer before becoming director of the Kaiser Wilhelm Institute for Chemistry in 1928. In 1938 Hahn discovered nuclear fission, which led to the production of nuclear power. For this prominent discovery of the fission of uranium and thorium he won the Nobel Prize in 1944. However, after seeing the results of Hiroshima and Nagasaki he became a vociferous opponent of these weapons.

Above: Sigmund Freud (1856–1939), the Austrian physiologist, medical doctor, and father of psychoanalysis, who is generally recognized as one of the most influential and authoritative thinkers of the twentieth century. Freud was born in Freiburg, Moravia, on May 6, but when he was four years old his family moved to Vienna, where Freud was to live and work until the last year of his life. Freud articulated and refined the concepts of the unconscious, of infantile sexuality, and of repression. In 1937 the Nazis annexed Austria, and Freud, who was Jewish, was allowed to leave for England. He died in London on September 23 days after war had been declared.

Above: An atomic bomb explodes in the lagoon of Bikini Atoll in the Marshall Islands. The site of 23 U.S. nuclear tests between 1946 and 1958, including the first hydrogen bomb, the inhabitants—who were removed in 1946—tried to return in 1972 but were evacuated because plutonium levels were still too dangerous.

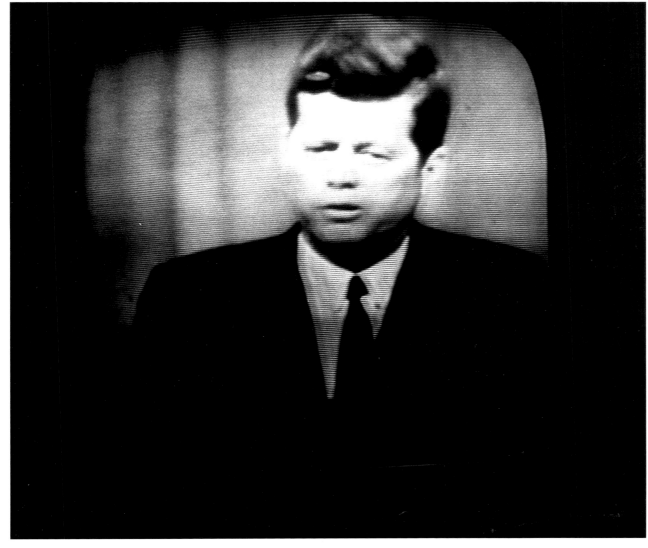

Above: This U.S. Department of Energy photograph shows the cloud from XX-58 IVY MIKE, an experimental thermonuclear device—or H-bomb—that was fired on Elugelab Island in the Eniwetok atoll on November 1,1952. The device used liquid deuterium as the fusion fuel and created a fireball three miles wide. The mushroom cloud rose to 57,000 ft in 90 seconds, and topped out in five minutes at 135,000 ft—the top of the stratosphere—with a stem eight miles across. The detonation completely obliterated Elugelab, leaving an underwater crater a 6,240ft wide and 164ft deep in the atoll where an island had once been.

Left: President John F Kennedy at his weekly Press conference in Washington, as viewers in Britain and Europe saw him when the conference was televised live via one of the first communications satellite, Telstar.

Above: Dr. Christiaan Barnard (1922–2001), the South African heart transplant pioneer. He died on September 2, 2001, at age 78. The cause of death was said to be a heart attack. Barnard performed the world's first successful heart transplant in December 1967.

Above: The technology of reproducing sound has changed considerably over the century—from records through tape to compact discs. Here a technician, Elmer Osaba of the Memorex factory in Santa Clara, California, is pictured checking the alignment of a tape reel destined to be split into 1/8th-inch widths for audio cassettes.

Above: What would Galileo think? Searching the heavens is no longer the province of optical telescopes. This is the "Very Large Array," one of the world's premier astronomical radio observatories, consists of 27 radio antennas in a Y-shaped configuration on the Plains of San Agustin 50 miles west of Socorro, New Mexico.

Left: Fifteen-year-old Louise Brown (born on July 25, 1978) was the first ever "test tube" baby. She is pictured with three-week old IVF twins Lauren (left) and Megan Miller. Louise weighed 5lb 12oz when she was born by Caesarian section to Mrs. Lesley Brown. She had been conceived in vitro—outside the mother's body.

Right: "It's good to talk!" Rose Coutts Smith at a photocall to launch the Cellnet mobile phone service in London. Pretty soon miniaturisation had reduced the size of the cell phone to more pocketable dimensions.

Above: One of the British Government advertisements in a £20 million anti-Aids campaign launched at the end of the twentieth century. Acquired Immune Deficiency Syndrome is the result of infection with Human Immune Deficiency—HIV. Originating in Africa, probably from the monkey population, mortality is high.

Right: Dolly the sheep, the world's first cloned adult animal, developed by a team at Edinburgh's Roslin Institute. This sort of scientific advance raises strong moral and ethical questions of scientists. How far should they trespass into areas many consider to be the province of God rather than humans?

Above: An employee of Motorola Electronics Taiwan displays the world's smallest and lightest mobile phone at the 1998 Taipei Telecommunication Show on September 15. The tiny telephone weighs 76g. Text messaging has now become the largest use for mobile communications.

Above Left: A Panasonic employee shows off a prototype DVD audio player and its DVD media at the Matsushita Electric Industrial Co. Ltd. booth in Audio Expo '98. The DVD audio media, with capacity of 4.7 or 8.5 gigabytes on a single side and 9.4 or 17 gigabytes in double-side, stores better quality sound than compact disc and was introduced to the markets in 1999.

Left: Viagra was touted as a miracle cure for male impotency and received FDA approval in the U.S. at the end of the century.

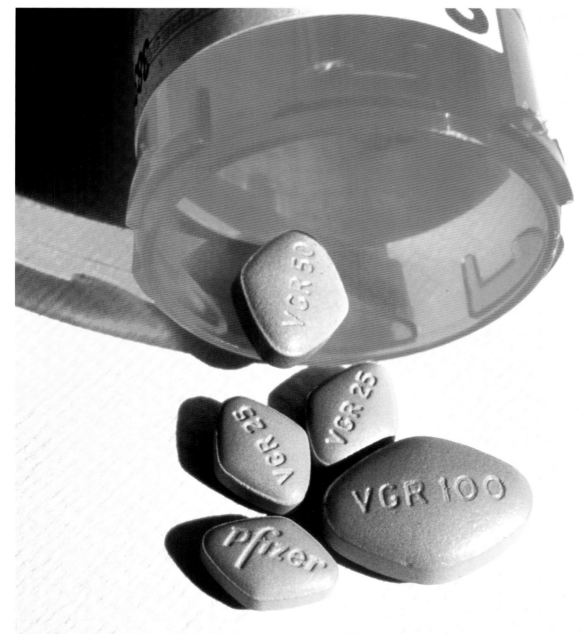

Above: U.S. President George W. Bush poses for photographers after making his nationwide address in which he backed federal funding for limited embryonic stem cell research August 9, 2001. Bush placed strict limits on how government monies are used on the promising but controversial science. "Embryonic stem cell research offers both great promise and great peril, so I've decided we must proceed with great care," Bush said.

Above Left: Computer toys—this picture taken at a department store in Tokyo, Japan, shows Japan's electronics giant Sony's new for the year 2000 robot pet.

Right: An Intel technician in Seattle holds a 12-inch wafer that contains hundreds of 3GHz Pentium 4 processors. The processors were the first to operate at the speed of three billion cycles per second. The speed of these processors defies belief and yet, mere months after arrival in the marketplace, they will be superseded.

Left: The growth of e-mail and personal computers meant that when the "I LOVE YOU" computer virus was started in 2000 it quickly spread worldwide through e-mail systems. The virus is believed to have originated in the Philippines.

Far Left: The first primate—Tetra, a female rhesus macaque monkey—cloned using a method that splits the original cells in an embryo to create multiple identical animals. The cloning took place at Schatten Lab at the Oregon Regional Primate Research Center in Beaverton.

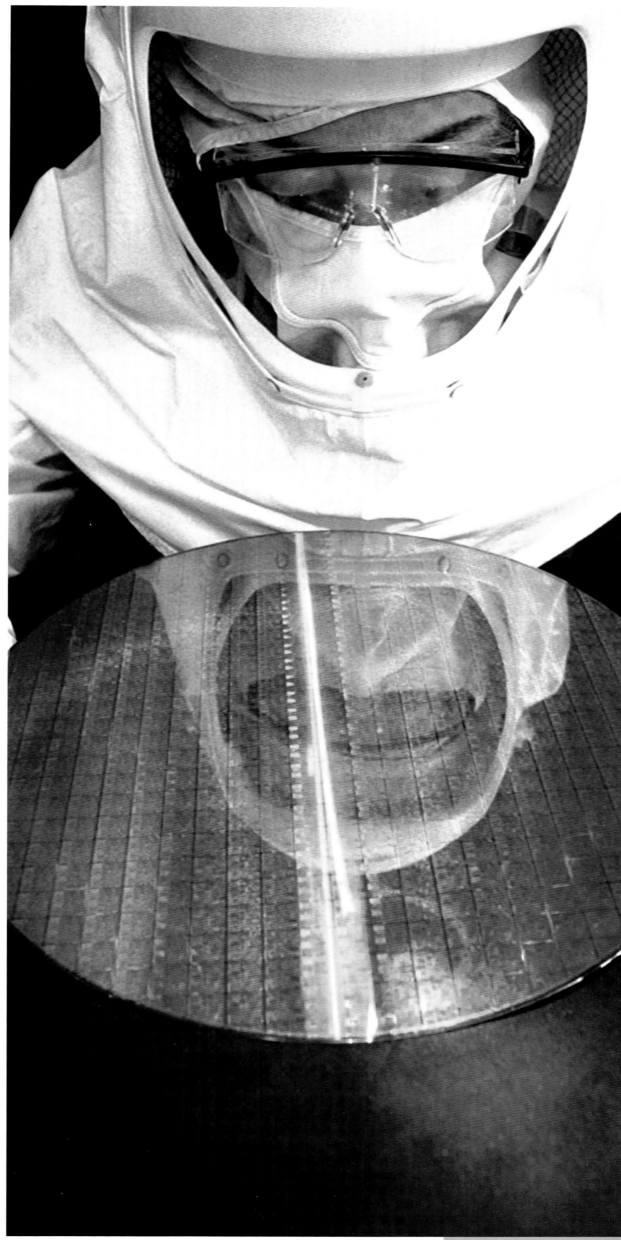

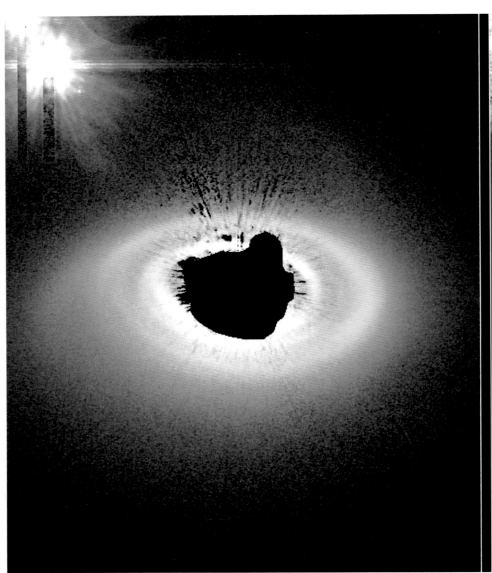

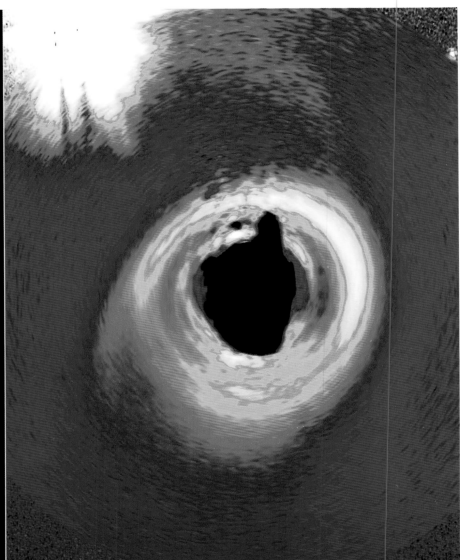

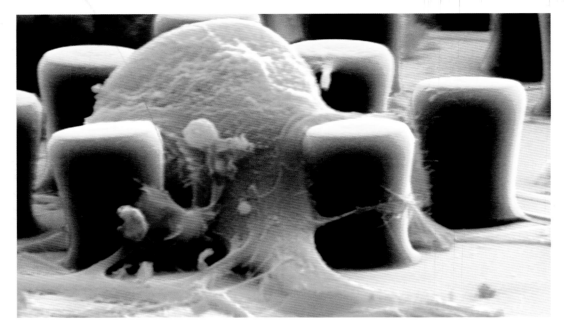

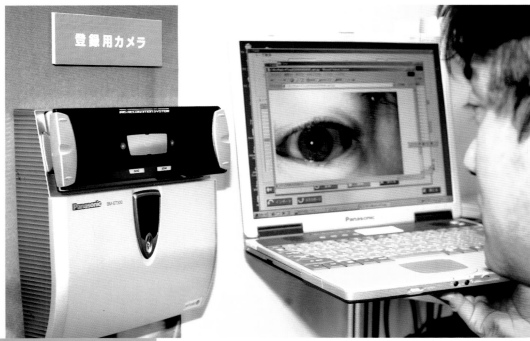

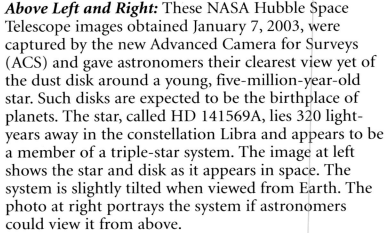

Above Left and Right: These NASA Hubble Space Telescope images obtained January 7, 2003, were captured by the new Advanced Camera for Surveys (ACS) and gave astronomers their clearest view yet of the dust disk around a young, five-million-year-old star. Such disks are expected to be the birthplace of planets. The star, called HD 141569A, lies 320 light-years away in the constellation Libra and appears to be a member of a triple-star system. The image at left shows the star and disk as it appears in space. The system is slightly tilted when viewed from Earth. The photo at right portrays the system if astronomers could view it from above.

Left: In a ground breaking experiment, scientists in Munich, Germany, attached a living nerve cell from the brain of a snail to a computer chip. The research by the Max Planck Institute showed that the cell and the chip can "talk" to each other by registering electrical impulses. This could be a giant breakthrough towards artificial retinas and prosthetic limbs, and brings the advent of the science fiction "cyborg" a stage nearer reality.

Left: Matsushita Electric unveiled a new biometric security system on iris recognition technology during Security Show 2003 in Tokyo, March 7, 2003. This technology enables the identification and authentication of each person by iris-pattern instead of password or fingerprint

Above: Solar energy collectors in Kleinulkow, a small village of 200 residents in eastern Germany, April 14, 2003. The first 13 units, each with 45 sq m of collectors, produce some 8,000 kW per unit. The energy collected is enough to supply a total of 45 families with energy. While it is unlikely that solar energy will replace fossil fuel for many years, it is one of a number of technologies that are vying for a lucrative, green marketplace.

Left: The ability to to put satellites into orbit around the earth has had a great effect on many areas of science—particularly communications and weather prediction. Satellite information has revolutionized mapping and a GPS—global positioning system—has brought satellite technology to the ordinary man in the street.

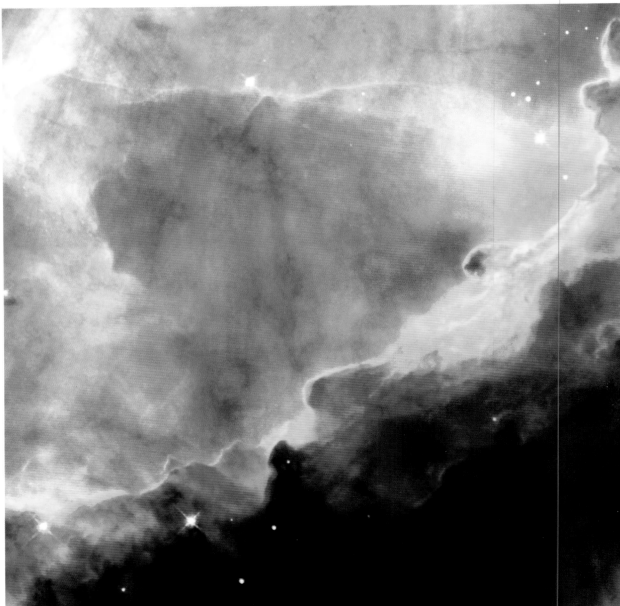

Above: Choirboys enter Hong Kong's Roman Catholic Cathedral wearing masks to protect against a killer pneumonia on Good Friday, April 18, 2003. The disease known as Severe Acute Respiratory Syndrome (SARS) caused widespread worldwide panic although, in relative terms, the death toll was light.

Above Right: NASA's Hubble Space Telescope has provided the world with remarkable photographs of deep space. This picture—taken by Hubble's Wide Field Planetary Camera 2 in May 1999— captures a small region within M17, a hotbed of star formation. M17, also known as the Omega or Swan Nebula, is located about 5,500 light-years away in the constellation Sagittarius and is roughly three light-years across. The image was released to commemorate the thirteenth anniversary of Hubble's launch on April 24, 1990.

Right: The new Liverpool telescope, the biggest robotic telescope in the world with a mirror of two meters' diameter, was inaugurated on Wednesday, May 7, 2003, on the island of La Palma.

Above: Humans have always tried to improve on nature and this device is no exception. Called the "Midgeater" it seeks to combat the biting summer pest that has terrorized locals and visitors to the banks of Loch Lomond in Scotland. Launched at the Loch Lomond Shores Visitor Centre, the sales blurb would have you believe that the reign of the midge over summer visitors to Scotland may be drawing to an end. If it were so then it would be a defining moment in any world history: only time will prove its efficacy.

Left: This photograph shows the world's first cloned mule, named Idaho Gem, at the University of Idaho in Moscow, ID, Friday, May 29, 2003. U.S. researchers have successfully cloned a mule, becoming the first to produce a clone in the horse family. The mule was born in April without complications, Gordon Woods, the leader of the research team that achieved the cloning, is quoted as saying in *New Scientist* magazine. Idaho Gem is a genetic copy of a prize-winning racing mule.

Left: A view across the hall of the experimental laboratory at the inner part of the nuclear research reactor FRM-II in Garching, Germany. The nuclear installation was officially started up by the Bavarian Premier Edmund Stoiber. The controversial facility is use by the University of Applied Sciences in Munich for research purposes. The nuclear reactor, which is a source for neutrons, sets worldwide a new benchmark for science and economy. The reactor is controversial because it uses nuclear weapon's grade uranium as fuel.

Right: The human-shaped Japanese robot Asimo (Advanced step in innovative mobility) applauds during his presentation at the Technical University Darmstadt on Monday, June 30, 2003. The 5ft-tall robot weighs over 260lb, can walk at just over a mile an hour and walk up stairs.

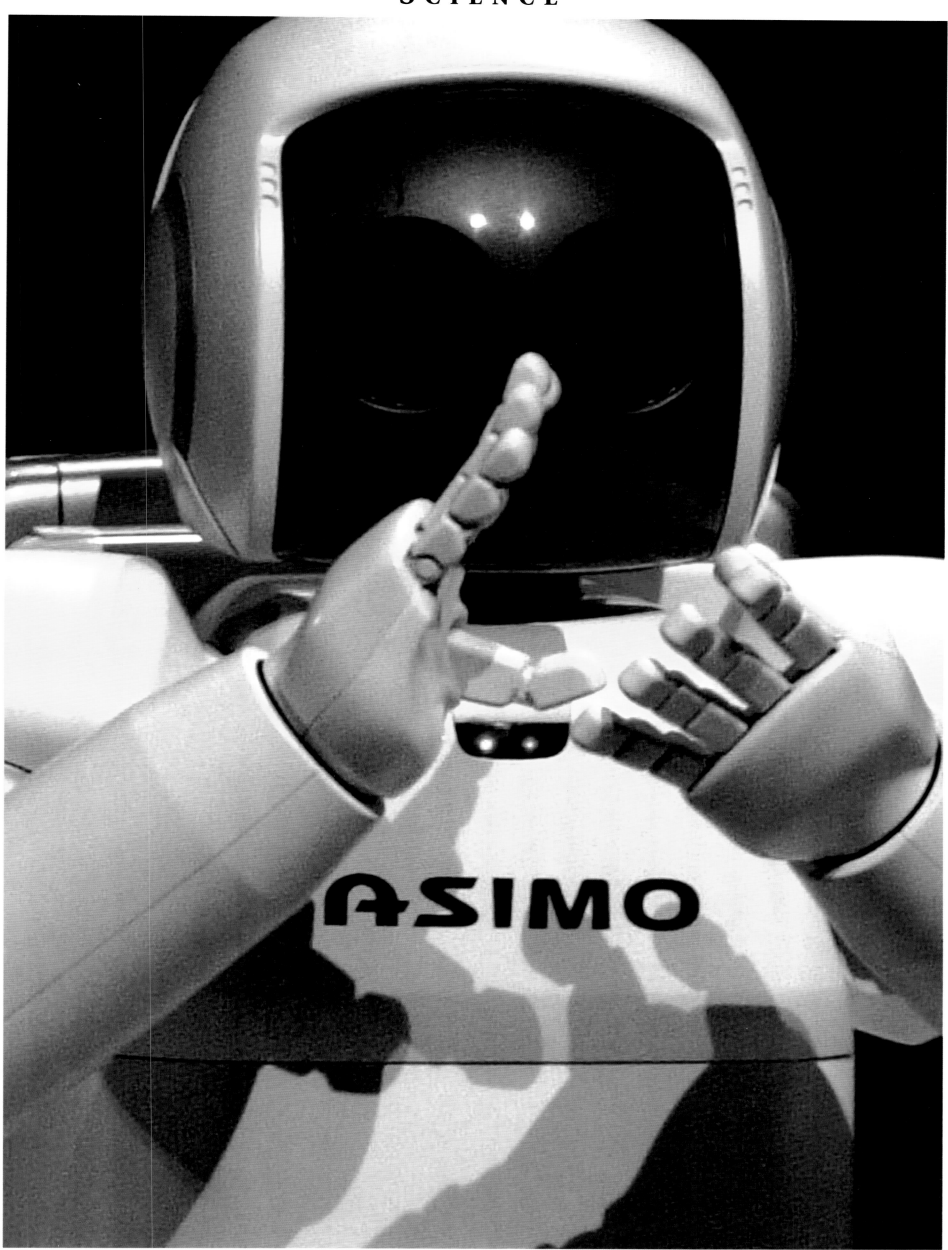

1932
Karl Jansky discovers radio static originating from the Milky Way. Radio astronomy becomes a new science.

1944
The V-2 rocket is developed by a German scientific team lead by Wernher von Braun.

1948
Largest telescope in the world at 5.08m located at Palomar Mountain, California.

1957
The USSR puts Laika the dog into space.
First satellite in space, Sputnik 1 launched by USSR; it transmits a tracking signal for 21 days.

1959
Monkeys return from space.
NASA launches Pioneer probes to the Moon. All fail.
USSR starts Luna program. Luna 2 crashlands on Moon surface. Luna 3 sends back photos of the Moon's far side.

1960
USSR dogs Belka and Strelka become first creatures to survive space when they return in Sputnik 5 after a day in orbit.
Distant star-like radio sources are discovered and named quasars. Their purpose and origin a mystery.

1961
Cosmonaut Yuri Gagarin becomes first man in space
Alan Shepard becomes first American in space.

1962
John Glenn becomes first man to orbit the Earth.
NASA's Mariner 2 probe passes Venus.
U.S. launches first communications satellite—Telstar.

1963
Soviet Valentina Tereshkova first woman in space
Maarten Schmidt measures the spectra of quasars.The first quasar is identified as 3C273.

1965
Cosmonaut Alexei Leonov takes the first space walk.
Astronaut Edward H White becomes first American to walk in space.
Early Bird becomes first commercially operated communications satellite.
Mariner 4 mission to Mars.
Big Bang Theory of the creation of the universe 13 billion years ago by Arno Penzias and Robert Wilson.

1966
Luna 9 probe soft lands on Moon surface.
U.S. astronauts dock in space.
NASA's Surveyor 1 successfully lands on Moon. Its mission to scout landing sites for manned mission.

1967
Apollo 1: fire aboard the space capsule on the ground at Cape Kennedy, Florida., kills astronauts Virgil I. Grissom, Edward H. White, and Roger Chaffee.
Soyuz 1: Vladimir M. Komarov killed when his craft crashes after its parachute lines, released at 23,000ft for reentry, became snarled.
First pulsar located by Jocelyn Bell Burnell and Anthony Hewish; identified as PSR 1919+21.

1968
Apollo 8 Orbits Moon.

1969
Apollo 11 lands on the Moon. Neil Armstrong becomes first man on the Moon.
U.S. Mariner 6 launched to Mars.
An infrared sky survey identifies 5,612 cool stars.

1970
NASA launches Uhuru satellite to use x-rays to map the skies. Finds over 300 x-ray sources including some possible black holes.
Apollo 13 on-board explosion leads to dramatic journey during which astronauts use the LEM as a lifeboat.
Soviet probe Venera 7 lands on Venus, but carries no camera and stops functioning within an hour.

1971
Soviet Salyut 1 become first space station.in orbit.
Soyuz 2: three cosmonauts, Georgi T. Dolrovolsky, Vladislav N. Volkov, and Viktor I. Patsayev, found dead in the craft after automatic landing.
Apollo14 lands on the Moon.
Soviet spacecraft docks with Salyut 1 space station.
Apollo15 lands the Lunar Roving Vehicle on the Moon. It surveys for 67 hours.

1972
Apollo 16 becomes last lunar landing mission. It stays

The Space Race was contested by two countries—the United States and the Soviet Union. Great prestige was at stake: national pride, international applause, and acknowledgement of scientific superiority. It was a race waged at the time of the Cold War and was taken to prove the superiority of the winner. But behind the rhetoric, both superpowers considered that whoever controlled the high skies—and in particular the space between Earth and the Moon—would control the Earth. Therefore the paranoia of both countries' military high commands became completely entangled in the space race. In the U.S., the Mercury Program was started with the intention of getting a man into space. Billions of dollars and rubles were poured into research and thousands were employed in the industry.

The Soviet Union was the first to launch an artificial satellite in 1957. Named "Sputnik" its launch was a worldwide sensation and it signaled the start of the Space Age. The first man into space was the Soviet Yuri Gagarin in Vostock I on April 12, 1961, soon followed by the American Alan Shepard on May 5, 1961. Both were propelled sling-shot style into space to fall straight back to Earth again. The first Earth orbit was made by Astronaut John Glenn on February 20, 1962, in the spaceship Friendship 7. (Glenn would later become the oldest man to visit space when, aged 77, he made his last flight on November 6, 1998.)

Astronomy is mostly a science of observation and calculation; space scientists can rarely touch the objects of their research. Most solar exploration has to be by unmanned probe and satellite. The first Solar System exploration was Mariner 2, in 1962. In addition to the Moon, all the nearest planets in our solar system have been studied, in particular Mars and Venus.

SPACE RACE

Following President John F Kennedy's vow on May 25, 1961, to put a man on the Moon, the Gemini Program started. After ten successful Gemini missions, it was superseded by Apollo—although not without incident: Apollo 1 burst into flames on the launch pad and three astronauts died. The first manned Apollo mission took place in October 1968; between then and 1972 the American space agency, NASA, carried out a brilliant program that saw man land on the Moon in 1969. A total of twelve men (from Apollo missions 11, 12, 14, 15, 16, and 17) have walked on the surface of the Moon.

The Soviets put their efforts into manned space stations named Salyut and Mir. In these cosmonauts undertook tours of many months' duration during which time they were carefully monitored. They conducted experiments and investigated and observed

the further reaches of space without the distortion caused by the Earth's atmosphere. Alexei Leonov was the first man to walk in space on March 18, 1965, and Valeri V. Polyakov holds the record for the longest period in space—437 days between January 8, 1994, and March 22, 1995.

All the while the exorbitant costs of space research caused both governments—particularly after the fall of the Communist regime in Russia—to cut back on their respective space programs. In a bid to save money, NASA developed and launched a reusable space orbiter—the first space shuttle. The cost of the shuttle launches was partially offset by their payload of satellites and experimental equipment such as the Hubble Space Telescope in 1990. The first shuttle flight was the orbiter *Columbia* between April 12–14, 1981. Many successful launches followed until disaster struck on January 28, 1986 when the shuttle *Challenger* exploded on take off. The program was badly set back and took a long time to revive.

for 75 hours—the longest yet.
Landsat 1 satellite launched to take infrared and visible photographs of the Earth's surface.

1973
Television pictures of Jupiter from the Pioneer 10 probe.
NASA launches Skylab.

1974
Mariner probe sends back photos of Mercury.
Discovery of first binary pulsar.

1975
Soviet probe Venera 9 lands on Venus and sends back photos of the surface before breaking down.
Apollo-Soyuz rendezvous in space—stay together for a few days on scientific experiments.

1976
NASA sends two Viking probes to Mars to photograph the planet, analyze rocks, and search for signs of life.

1977
NASA sends two Voyager space probes to the outer planets. They send back photos and data from Jupiter and Saturn.
NASA tests the Space Shuttle.
Work starts to build the Hubble Space Telescope.

1980
Soviet Vostok rocket explodes on the launch pad while being refueled. Kills 50 at the Plesetsk Space Center.

1981
Maiden flight of Columbia, the first Space Shuttle

1983
IRAS, first infrared astronomy satellite launched. Maps 98% of the sky over 300 days before its fuel runs out. Discovers 250,000 cosmic infrared sources.

1984
U.S. astronauts make first untethered space walk.

1986
Voyager 2 passes Uranus and Neptune.
On January 31, Challenger Space Shuttle explodes 73 seconds after lift off, killing all seven crew members: Francis R. Scobee, Michael J. Smith, Judith A. Resnick, Ronald E. McNair, Ellison S. Onizuka, Gregory B. Jarvis, and schoolteacher Christa McAuliffe.
NASA space flight program halted for almost three years for inquiries and modifications.
Halley's Comet passes Earth.
European Space Agency's probe Giotto flies through the comet and photographs the nucleus.

1986
Launch of Soviet Mir space station.

1990
NASA's Magellan space probe reaches Venus, its three-year mission to map the planet with radar.
Hubble Space Telescope launched using the Space Shuttle, but suffers crucial damage to its mirror.
The Rosat survey finds over 1,000 extreme ultraviolet hot stars.

1992
COBE (Cosmic Background Explorer) satellite produces map showing cosmic "ripples" indicating the remnants of the background radiation from the Big Bang.
Keck Telescope on Mauna Kea, Hawaii is completed, the first of a new generation of optical telescope.

1993
Costly repair mission restores Hubble Space Telescope. Amazing photos of galaxies, nebulas, stars, and deep space are returned to Earth for analysis.

1995
Space probe Galileo arrives to survey Jupiter.
Hubble photos the birth of a star—in the Eagle Nebula

1996
NASA's Space Shuttle Atlantis docks with Soviet MIR space station.

1998
Construction starts on an international space station. John Glenn becomes the oldest man to visit space when he flew on a Space shuttle mission age 77.

2001
U.S. millionaire Dennis Tito becomes first space tourist, visiting the International Space Station aboard a Russian booster.

2003
On February 1 the Space Shuttle Columbia explodes and breaks up on Earth's atmosphere killing all seven crew members: Rick D. Husband, William C. McCool, Michael P. Anderson, David M. Brown, Kalpana Chawla, Laurel Clark, and the first Israeli, Ilan Ramon.

Left: Laika the dog, was the first living creature in space when she was launched in Sputnik 2. She survived the launch but died when the oxygen ran out while in orbit.

Below: Cosmonaut Major Yuri Gagarin (1934–68) became a hero as the first man in space. His spaceship, the spherical Vostok, completed a circuit 344km above the Earth lasting 108 minutes. He was made a Hero of the Soviet Union and shared the Galabert Astronautical prize with John Glenn in 1963. Here he smiles as he waves goodbye to the cheering thousands seeing him off as he boards a Russian airliner at London airport to fly home to the Soviet Union after a visit to Great Britain. Sadly, Gagarin was killed in an aircraft accident a few years later while training for his return to space. A crater on the Moon is named in memory of him.

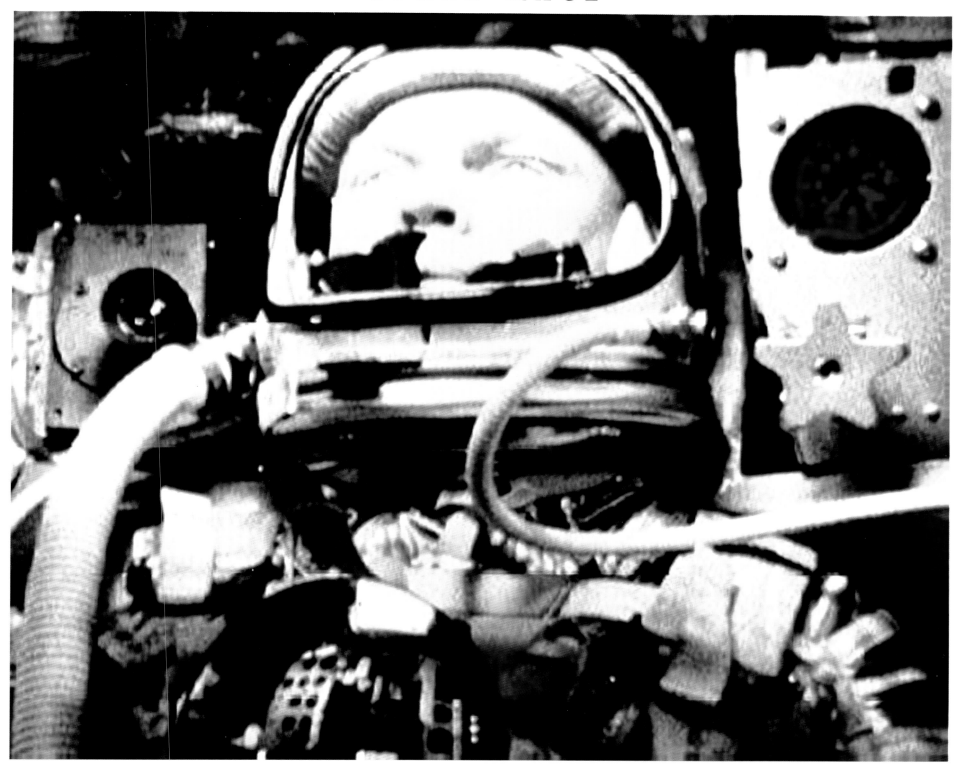

Above: John Glenn in Friendship 7 while orbiting the Earth on February 1, 1962. He made three orbits during a five-hour flight. He retired from NASA in 1964 and the Marine Corps in 1965 and stood for election to the Senate ten years later. He was returned as Democratic senator for his home state of Ohio. He returned to space age 77 when he joined a Shuttle mission in 1998.

Left: The Russian President Vladimir Putin meeting cosmonauts at the space training center in Zvezdny Gorodok (Star City) near Moscow, in April 2001. There he met Valentina Tereshkova, the first woman in space and Peter Klimuk (left) the head of the cosmonaut training center. Built in 1960 Star City hosts the Yuri Gagarin Cosmonaut Training Center named in honor of its first and most famous graduate.

Right: Astronaut Edwin ("Buzz") Aldrin with the Stars and Stripes proudly planted on the surface of the Moon, July 21, 1969. The second man to walk on the Moon, "Buzz" Aldrin was the pilot of Apollo 11. Together with Neil Armstrong, Aldrin spent 22 hours on the lunar surface and two and a half hours outside the lunar module Eagle during which time they collected 22kg of Moon samples. Aldrin had already made the space history books in November 1966, when he recorded a five-hour space walk during the Gemini 12 mission.

Left: The moon was starkly beautiful—no one who watched Armstrong's first steps could fail to be moved by the experience.

Below: After their triumphant visit to the Moon, the three Apollo 11 astronauts became international heroes. To show themselves to the world they embarked on a whirlwind 38-day tour of 22 countries. From left to right: Edwin "Buzz" Aldrin, Neil Armstrong, and Michael Collins seen just before they left London to fly to Rome, on October 15, 1969.

EDWIN E. ALDRIN, JR.   NEIL A.

Left: This artist's rendition shows Pioneer 10, the first spacecraft to travel through the asteroid belt and the first spacecraft to make direct observations and obtain close-up images of Jupiter. Famed as the most remote object ever made by man, Pioneer 10, launched March 2, 1972, is now over 7.4 billion miles away.

Above: The Space Shuttle *Discovery* takes off from Launch Pad 39B at the Kennedy Space Center, Florida, at 11:37:00a.m. EDT on September 29, 1988. The 26th shuttle mission lasted just over four days, landing on October 3, 1988, at Edwards Air Force Base, California. Its primary payload, NASA Tracking and Data Relay Satellite-3 (TDRS-3) attached to an Inertial Upper Stage (IUS), became the second TDRS deployed. After deployment, IUS propelled the satellite to a geosynchronous orbit. The crew consisted of Frederick H. Hauck, Commander; Richard O. Covey, Pilot; John M. Lounge, Mission Specialist 1; George D. Nelson, Mission Specialist 2; and David C. Hilmers, Mission Specialist 3.

Below: December 7, 1972—the huge, 363-feet tall Apollo 17 space vehicle is launched from Kennedy Space Center, Florida, at 12:33 a.m. (EST). Apollo 17, the final lunar landing mission in the Apollo program, was the first nighttime liftoff of the Saturn V launch vehicle. Aboard Apollo 17 were Eugene A. Cernan, commander; Ronald E. Evans, command module pilot; and Harrison H. Schmitt, lunar module pilot. Flame from the five F-1 engines of the Apollo/Saturn first stage illuminates the nighttime scene. A two-hour and forty-minute hold delayed the Apollo 17 launching.

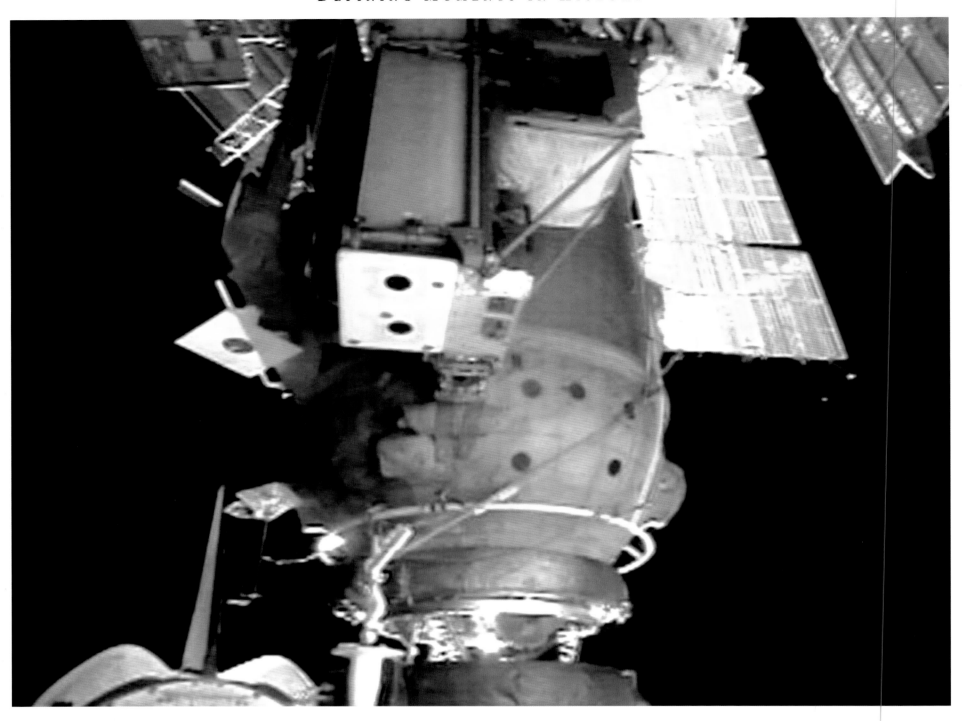

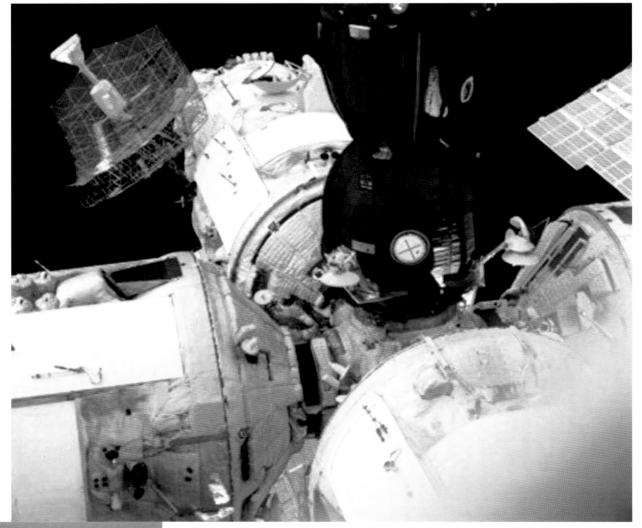

Above: The docking module of the Russian Space Station Mir is shown here as it makes contact with the Space Shuttle *Atlantis*' docking ring, late January 14, 1997. The *Atlantis* remained docked with Mir for five days of joint science operations and to replace U.S. Astronaut John Blaha with U.S. Astronaut Jerry Linenger on the station.

Above Right: A sunset from space as seen by the crew of the Space Shuttle *Discovery* on August 14 from one of the shuttle's aft flightdeck windows. The *Discovery* and her six-person crew were into flight-day eight of their 11-day science mission.

Left and Right: The Russian Mir space station seen from *Atlantis*, January 16, 1997.

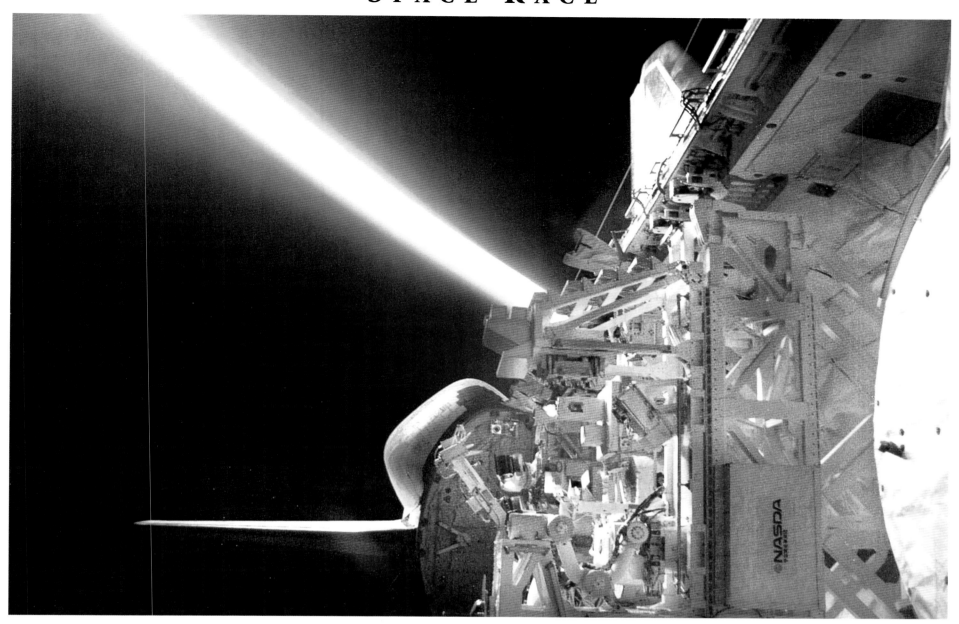

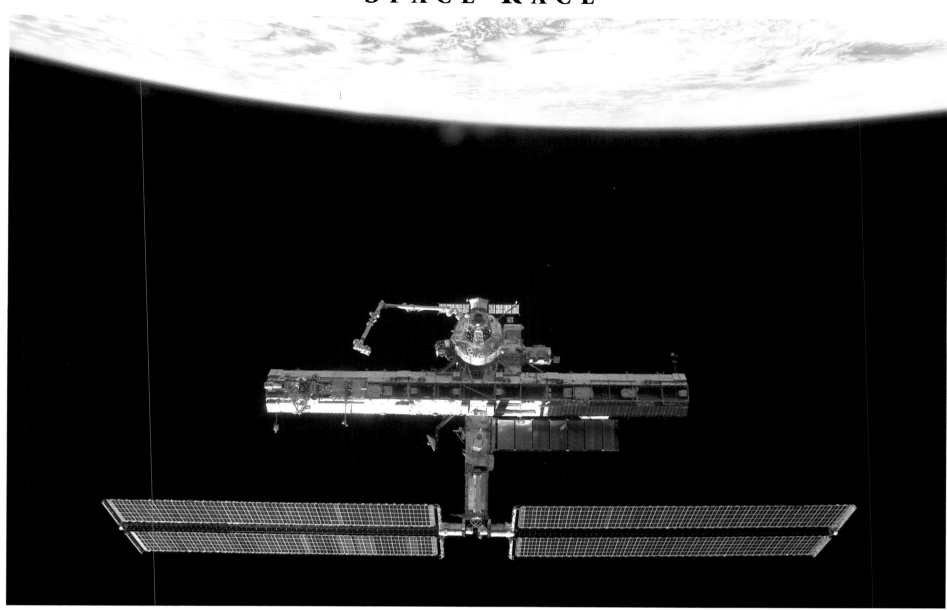

Above Left: *Columbia* deploys her drag chute upon landing at runway 33, Kennedy Space Center, Florida, July 27, 1999. The *Columbia* and her five-person crew's five-day included the release of the Chandra X-ray telescope.

Left: Astronaut Carlos I. Noriega waves as his space walk partner, astronaut Joseph R. Tanner, takes his photo during the second of three sessions of extravehicular activity (EVA).

Above: The International Space Station as seen from the U.S. space shuttle *Endeavour* as the shuttle undocks and moves away, December 2, 2002, shows. The complex has a three-seater Russian Soyuz vehicle docked to it in case of emergencies.

Right: This artist's rendition showing the SIRTF (Space Infrared Telescope Facility) satellite orbiting the Sun. SIRTF was launched into space from Cape Canaveral, Florida on April 15, 2003. During its 2.5-year mission, SIRTF will obtain images and spectra by detecting the infrared energy, or heat, radiated by objects in space.

Above: The Russian Soyuz TMA-2 rocket carrying Russian cosmonaut Yuri Malenchenko and U.S. astronaut Edward Lu, blasts off from the Baikonur cosmodrome, Kazakhstan, April 26, 2003. In the first space flight since the *Columbia* shuttle disaster three months earlier, the rocket docked with the International Space Station. Today's cooperation contrasts strikingly with the Cold War space race.

Far Right: Space is not just the province of Russia and the U.S. Here, a Russian Soyuz-FG medium-class rocket-carrier takes off from Baikonur on June 3, 2003 with the European Space Agency's Mars Express spacecraft aboard. The launch proceeded successfully.

Right: Scientists working on the Shenzhou V manned spacecraft in Beijng, May 8, 2003.

Left: The Mobile Service Tower is rolled back at Launch Complex 17A, Cape Canaveral Air Force Station, to reveal a Delta II rocket ready to launch the Mars Exploration Rover-A (MER-A) mission, Sunday, June 8, 2003. NASA officials postponed the launching of the spaceship due to heavy rains in the area. The cost of spaceflight, the machinery, and instrumentation put together for a mission such as this means that every care is taken to ensure a safe take off. The MER missions are yet another example of the advanced technology employed in space. NASA's twin Mars Exploration Rovers are designed to study the history of water on Mars. Each rover could travel as far as 100 meters in one day to act as Mars scientists' eyes and hands.

Right: Blue sky and sun are the backdrop for a flawless launch of MER-A, known as "Spirit," on Tuesday, June 10, 2003. When the two rovers arrive at Mars in 2004, they will bounce to airbag-cushioned landings at sites offering a balance of favorable conditions for safe landings and interesting science. The rovers see sharper images, can explore farther and examine rocks better than anything that has ever landed on Mars. The designated site for the MER-A mission is Gusev Crater, which appears to have been a crater lake. The second rover, MER-B, launched at the end of June 2003.

The first transport revolution took place in the nineteenth century as mass transit was required as heavy industry grew. First canals, then railroads spread out all over the world. In the United States, by the 1840s there were more than 3,000 miles of rail. By the eve of the Civil War network was more than 30,000 miles long, and the railroads of the western lines had nearly caught up with the ever-moving western frontier. Following the Civil War several lines were extended all the way to the Pacific coast, the first being the Union Pacific-Central Pacific, completed in 1869. As industrial development reached Asia, Africa, South America, and Australia, railways appeared on those continents. By the early decades of the 20th century, nearly 900,000 miles of railroad had been built in the world, with some mileage in nearly every nation. In North America, for example, the lineage was huge: by 1890 the length of the US rail system was

163,000 miles; by 1916 it had reached an all-time high of 254,000 miles. Today the figure is nearer 150,000.

Early in the century the monopoly that had been held by railroads was challenged by a number of new modes of transport: thousands and soon millions of private automobiles; intercity buses; larger and larger trucks; airplanes carrying mail, passengers, and high-priority freight; and a growing network of pipelines. As a result, railways in the United States and Europe went into decline after World War I, with substantial losses in mileage, employment, and traffic. The invention of the internal combustion engine in Europe had led to the second transport revolution—that of personal mobility. Individual manufacturers started making small numbers of automobiles for a select group of wealthy customers but it was Henry Ford who devised factory-line mass-production and cars became cheap enough for ordinary people to own. Manufacture of the Model T stopped in 1929 by which time a grand

TRANSPORT

total of 16,536,075 had been made in America alone (more were made under licence in England and Canada). In America The Ford Motor Company and General Motors soon filled the roads with automobiles. They were so successful with promoting their product that by 1929 nearly half a million people were employed in Detroit and the automobile industry was the largest and most successful in the country with 4.5 million cars manufactured that year. In 1929 nearly 27 million vehicles were registered in the US (today the figure is nearer 200 million)—governments around the world had been quick to spot the revenue-raising potential of motor vehicles. This phenomenal growth in personal transportation necessitated the consequent investment in new and better roads. Government and private companies embarked on a massive road building program that continues to this day.

The most incredible development in the 20th century, however, was that of flight. The first powered flight is credited to Orville Wright in North Carolina in 1902; he and his brother Wilbur set up an aircraft production company in 1909 but it was not until World War I when serious money from governments was invested into engine and airframe development. As flight technology improved more investment was allocated for airplanes, especially military fighters. Similar ground-breaking technical advances were made during World War II including the invention of the jet engine. The demand for transcontinental passenger trade led to the founding of dedicated services and huge leaps in aircraft technology—such as the quantum leap forward provided by Boeing 747 Jumbo Jet in 1970. Supersonic passenger travel became scheduled for the first time in January 1976 with the British Airways and Air France Concorde. To accommodate these aircraft, airports opened up and by the turn of the century the Unites States could boast over 14,000, some way ahead of Brazil, the next in the league table with around 3,000.

American Airlines launched as successor to American Airways.

1935
DC-3 introduced, one of the most successful airliners of all time.
Moscow underground opens; it will become the busiest in the world by the end of the century.
Launch of the Normandie. She will be destroyed by fire in New York Harbor as USS Lafayette having been seized by the US government on its entry into WWII.

1937
Volkswagen Beetle first produced. By the end of the century it will be the second (after the Corolla) bestselling model ever.
Golden Gate Bridge completed (main span 4,200ft).

1938
Howard Hughes goes round world in 3 days 19hr 17min.

1947
Nationalization of Britain's rail companies.

1952
World's first scheduled commercial flight by a jet-propeled aircraft, the Comet.
SS United States wins Blue Riband with a 3 day 10hr 40min Atlantic crossing.

1954
St. Lawrence Seaway commenced

1955
A Comet III circles the globe in 2 days 18hr 43min flying time.

1958
Last British steam locomotive constructed.

1959
Hovercraft invented by Christopher Cockerill.

1961
Last journey of the Orient Express from Paris to Budapest

1963
Publication of the Beeching report on British Railways recommending cutting one third of the track and half the stations.

1966
Toyota Corolla first produced. By 2000 over 23 million will have been built—the most of any model.

1967
X15 reaches fastest recorded speed by piloted aircraft in the earth's atmosphere—4,520mph

1968
End of steam on British rail system.

1969
Boeing 747 first flight
Concorde inaugural flight
Launch of the QE2.
Czechoslovakia makes seatbelt wearing compulsory—the first country to do so.

1971
Formation of AMTRAK.

1974
The first Air France Airbus goes into service on the Paris-London route.

1977
Gossamer Condor wins the Kremer Prize for the first man-powered flight.
The longest steel arch bridge (at 1,700 feet) opens over the New River Gorge at Fayetteville, West Virginia.

1986
A microlight aircraft circles Earth nonstop.

1990
The Channel Tunnel between England and France opens.

1997
Thrust sets the first supersonic land speed record.

2000
Launch of Explorer of the Seas, sister of 1999 launched Voyager of the Seas. These Finnish-built cruise ships carry nearly 4,000 passengers each—the largest ever.
The longest (at over 15 miles) road tunnel—the Laerdal—opens in Norway.

Above: Wright's glider. Orville (1871–1948) and Wilbur (1867–1912) Wright worked together in a bicycle shop before they became the first to fly in a heavier than air machine. After doing so they started manufacturing aircraft and sold the first military aircraft in the world to the U.S. Signal Corps in 1908.

Right: The Honourable Charles Stewart Rolls (1877–1910), pioneer motorist and aviator, with an early type of triplane at Shellbeach, England. In 1906 he went into partnership with Henry Royce

Left: October 1, 1908. Henry Ford, US car manufacturer, poses for a photographer in his new Model T Ford in front of his car plant in Detroit. Henry Ford, who produced his first petrol-driven car in 1893, confirmed his status as America's greatest inventor in 1913 by setting up the first moving assembly line.

TRANSPORT

Left: Wilbur and Orville Wright at Sheppey England, January 1, 1912. At the height of the brothers' success, Wilbur died of typhoid in 1912. Orville sold his share in the company in 1915 to concentrate on research.

Below: Britain's first submarine Holland I supported in dry dock at Portsmouth after being retrieved from the seabed. She sank on her way to the breakers' yard in 1913.

Above: The son of a Polish Count and an American mother, Louis Zboroswki lived near Canterbury where he built three aero-engined cars, all called Chitty Bang Bang. He raced both in Europe and America. A colourful character and an excellent driver, his career was cut short before his thirtieth birthday.

Above: Duke and Duchess of York aboard H.M.S. Renown pass through the Panama Canal in 1927, some 12 years after the canal opened to commercial traffic. The *Renown*, in company with the *Repulse*, was sunk by Japanese aircraft in 1941.

Above: Charles Lindbergh (1902–74) seen on May 21, 1927, with *Spirit of Saint Louis*—the aircraft in which he made the first non-stop flight across the Atlantic from New York to Paris.

Above: Amelia Earhart (1897–1937), the first woman to fly the Atlantic (in 1932) and the first person to fly alone from Hawaii to California (1935). She disappeared in the Pacific in 1937 while on a solo round the world flight.

Above: The German airship *Graf Zeppelin* after her maiden flight. On August 29, 1929, the airship made history when she flew around the globe in 21 days, 7 hr and 26 min.

TRANSPORT

Left: The German leader Adolf Hitler sits in the back as he inspects the first Volkswagen Beetle produced in Stuttgart in 1937. Nazi Party officials look on. By the end of the century it will be the second (after the Corolla) bestselling model ever.

Right: The world's first jet airliner, the De Havilland Comet, making her first flight from Hatfield, Hertfordshire, July 27, 1949. It would enter commercial service in 1952. A spate of unexplained accidents in the mid-1950s would see it grounded for a critical period and lose out on sales to American rivals.

Left: Miss Amy Johnson (1903–41), London Aeroplane Club, is the first woman to gain an Air Ministry's ground engineer's licence, January 10, 1930, relates the original caption to this photograph. A qualified pilot, Amy Johnson flew solo from England to Australia and won £10,000 from a newspaper for doing so. During the war she flew for the Air Transport Auxiliary and died after baling out over the Thames estuary.

Right: This Bell X-1A flown by "Chuck" Yeager (1903–) was the first to fly twice the speed of sound. Yeager had broken the sound barrier on October 14, 1947, being dropped in an X-1 called *Glamorous Glennis* (after his wife) from the belly of a B-29 bomber. He would say of the event: "I'm still wearing my ears, and nothing else fell off, neither." Those waiting on the ground, however, were keyed up because of the uncertainties about the flight, and the world's first sonic boom took most of them by surprise. "They didn't understand — they thought something had blown up." He went to Vietnam as a wing commander in 1966 and flew over 120 combat missions. In 1986, Yeager was appointed to the Presidential Commission investigating the *Challenger* accident.

Above: It's June 17, 1957. Steam has only another 10 years to run on Britain's railways. The photograph shows the inauguration of the "Caledonian," an express from London's Euston station to Glasgow, Scotland's second city. Seen thundering through Watford on the long haul of some 400 miles to Glasgow on her inaugural run northbound, the train's schedule called for an average speed of more than 60mph. On the reverse run from Glasgow to London the "Caledonian," set up a postwar record for the trip of 398 minutes.

Left: After many years of faithful service, steam-haulage made its last appearance on the Britain's crack, all-Pullman, "Golden Arrow" boat train, June 11, 1961. The "Golden Arrow" nameboard is removed by fitters at London's Victoria station: tomorrow it will leave London behind a powerful electric locomotive.

Above: This photograph shows NASA's venerable B-52 mothership taken from a KC-135 tanker aircraft. The X-43 adapter is visible attached to the right wing. The B-52, used for launching experimental aircraft and for other flight research projects, has been a familiar sight in the skies over Edwards for more than 40 years and is also both the oldest B-52 still flying and the aircraft with the lowest flight time of any B-52.

Right: Conceived as a triple-sonic interceptor, the YF-12 had all of the blazing performance of its more famous sister aircraft, the SR-71. On May 1, 1965, the YF-12 set no less than nine world absolute speed and altitude records at Edwards AFB. Among these was a sustained altitude of 80,257ft and a speed of 2,070mph. In spite of this performance and operational potential, the aircraft never entered production.

Above: Donald Campbell's *Bluebird K7* hydroplane at speed on Coniston Water, England, January 4, 1967. Campbell died when his jet-powered boat, *Bluebird K7*, flipped over and crashed as he tried to break his own world water speed record on Coniston Water, in the Lake District. In 2000, divers finally found the submerged wreck of *Bluebird K7*, 34 years after Campbell was killed.

Left: Alec Issigonis, creator of the British Motor Corporation's Mini car range, drives the millionth Mini off the production line at the Austin Plant at Longbridge, Birmingham on February 2, 1965.

Right: On December 1, 1990, Britain was connected with the European mainland for the first time since the ice age, as tunnelers broke through to the French side. This milestone was reached during the building of the Channel Tunnel when the final underground section between the Kent coast and the terminal site broke through. The workers are pictured celebrating their arrival in Folkestone.

TRANSPORT

Above: The launch of the newly named *Queen Elizabeth 2* by her Majesty the Queen at John Brown's Yard, Clydebank. The name of the new Cunard liner was kept secret until the launch on September 20, 1967.

Above: Concorde 002 shoots away skyward on its first supersonic test flight over land from Fairford, September 1, 1970.

Left: This NASA photograph dated November 1998 shows the *Centurion* flying wing over the California desert near Edwards, CA. The *Centurion* is a remotely piloted solar powered flying wing which is designed to reach altitudes of 90,000 to 100,000ft to conduct atmospheric sampling and other science missions.

Below: Inventor Dean Kamen debuts the Segway Human Transporter (HT), which his company, Segway LLC, describes as "a self-balancing electric-powered transportation machine," during a news conference in New York December 3, 2001. The Segway HT was designed for use in cities by providing a solution to short-distance travel.

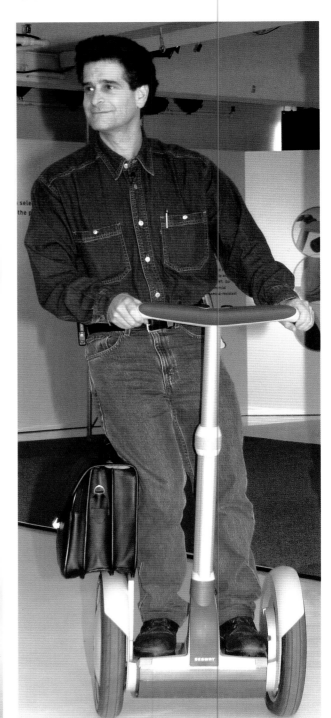

Above: The Italian-built module, US Node 2, for the International Space Station, is offloaded from a Beluga at the Shuttle Landing Facility at Cape Canaveral Air Station, Florida June 2, 2003. US Node 2 attaches to the end of the US Lab and provides attach locations for the Japanese laboratory, European laboratory, the Centrifuge Accommodation Module, and, later, Multipurpose Logistics Modules. It will provide the primary docking location for the Shuttle when a pressurized mating adapter is attached to Node 2. Installation of the module will complete the US core of the station.

Above Right: Pilot Alexia Cortese of the Ecam team, steers her "Solifuge 2,0" prototype during the Brussels Eco Week-End, Saturday, June 28, 2003, in Brussels. The prototype cars taking part in this particular race are developed to run a maximum distance with minimum benzine. The world record in this speciality is held by a car developed by Mazda which raced 2,050km (c1,280 miles) with only one liter (just over two pints) of benzine.

Right: A magnetically-levitated train carrying some 50 visitors, speeds on its test track on August 20, 1999 in Tsuru city, near Tokyo. The Central Japan Railway held the three-day 600-people family ride on the "Maglev" train, which set a world speed record of 552km/hr (342mph).

1913
Federal Reserve Act passed to control US monetary policy, establish the money supply, and supervise international banking.

1923
In January German mark plummets to 20,000 to the dollar. By November it is worth 630,000 million.

1928
Dow Jones Industrial average index reorganized and given the value of 100.

1929
October 29, Wall Street Stock Exchange crash. Many causes including wild stockmarket speculation, inadequate reserves, high protectionist tariffs, and manufacture outstripping consumption.

1930
Publication of A Treatise on Money by John Maynard Keynes about a planned economy.

1932
President Hoover creates the Reconstruction Finance Corporation to try to break the Great Depression.
July 2. Dow Jones Index hits all-time low of 41.

1933
Franklin D. Roosevelt's "New Deal." In the following 100 days Congress passed legislation designed to improve the US economy.
The Glass-Steagal Act prohibits universal banking in the US.

1936
Publication of revolutionary economic work General Theory of Employment, Interest and Money by John Maynard Keynes.

1944
Bretton Woods Conference, New Hampshire leads to the establishment of the International Monetary System and the International Monetary Fund (IMF), and the World Bank. Agreement signed by 45 nations.

1945
International Bank for Reconstruction and Development (IBRD) founded to help raise standards of living in developing countries. aka World Bank.

1947
European Recovery Program, aka Marshall Aid. US financial aid to war damaged Europe, named for US Secretary of State George Marshall.

1949
Devaluation of the pound sterling in Britain with intention of making exports cheaper and imports more expensive so as to improve currency reserves.
First quotes from the Nikkei Stock Average (known then as Nikkei Dow Jones Index) from the Tokyo Stock Exchange.

1956
Milton Friedman, Professor of Economics at Chicago, produces a study of quantity theory and begins modern monetarism.

1957
Treaty of Rome establishes the European Common Market. Original signatories: Belgium, France, Italy, West Germany, Luxembourg, and the Netherlands.

1960
The ATM (automated teller machine), aka cash dispenser, invented by Luther Simjian.
Formation of OPEC—Organization of the Petroleum Exporting Countries.

1961
Organization for Economic Cooperation and Development (OECD) formed to assist member countries formulate policies to achieve high economic growth while keeping financial stability.
United Nations Industrial Development Organization (UNIDO) formed to promote industrialization of developing countries, especially in manufacturing.

1964
First quote from the Hang Seng Index, based on the capital value of 33 stocks on the Hong Kong Stock Exchange.

oney makes the world go round and the capitalist world in particular is susceptible to the machinations of the money markets. The international currency of the early half of the twentieth century was gold. Countries stockpiled gold and other precious metals—most famously at Fort Knox in Kentucky, the site of the US Bullion Depository and the Bank of England in the City of London. With such gold reserves countries could negotiate deals with both sides knowing that the necessary funds were sitting safely in their vaults. This situation changed as technology and in particular the motor vehicle started using more and more oil and gasoline. Oil became the international currency that everyone wanted and needed. The oil producing countries of the world suddenly came to the fore as big hitters in the world economy.

Much of the world oil reserves were discovered in the Middle East and the countries there that found themselves suddenly important and wealthy formed themselves into the Organization of Petroleum Exporting Countries (OPEC) in 1960. There were five founder members, Iran, Iraq, Kuwait, Saudi Arabia, and Venezuela (later joined by eight more countries). Set up to fix the price for crude oil and co-ordinate policy between its members, OPEC has used its muscle to great effect and the member countries have got fabulously wealthy as a result.

The 1920s and 1930s were dominated by the international economy. The upheaval of World War I left European economies devastated by war debt and Germany in particular suffered most with the heavy demand of reparations. In January 1923 the German mark went into freefall and depreciated to 20,000 to the dollar, but this was only the start, it kept falling and by August the rate was to five million, then in early November it dropped to a staggering 630,000 million. For all practical purposes the mark was worthless. The result was complete economic breakdown, even daily revision could not

Economics

keep up with the plummeting mark. Savings, pensions, wages, mortgages, debts and all paper investments including foreign investment were wiped out.

The next great economic disaster hit Wall Street on October 24, 1929, known as "Black Thursday" when the price of stocks and shares started to slide downward. Fuelled by wild stock market speculation and manufacture outstripping consumption (among other things) confidence evaporated and wild selling of stocks and shares ensued. But by Tuesday 29, October the stock market had completely panicked and the market imploded. Businesses, investors, and people were ruined. The result was the Great Depression that lasted for ten years before President Franklin D. Roosevelt managed to turn the economy around.

The United States suffered most but countries around the world felt the repercussions. The money markets are fickle and they flex and fall sometimes for no apparent reason. After economic boom in the early 1980s the bust came on "Black Monday" in April 1987. Since then politicians, economists, and bankers have attempted to install checks and balances to prevent such lurches in the economy. They still happen, but so far not as dramatically as previously. Fraud on a massive scale unnerves the markets, such as news of the bogus accounting used company-wide by the huge Enron Corporation that broke December 2001. Enron and their accountants Arthur Andersen colluded to present accounts that showed that Enron were one of the biggest and most profitable companies in the world. This was so far from the truth that Enron was forced to file for bankruptcy on December 2, 2001. Such colossal fraud from such a major player was half expected to presage an economic collapse but in this instance the markets worked hard to stabilize themselves although other companies have since been discovered to have followed similar false accounting methods.

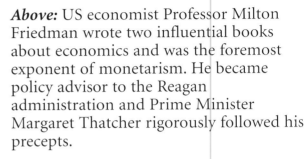

Above: US economist Professor Milton Friedman wrote two influential books about economics and was the foremost exponent of monetarism. He became policy advisor to the Reagan administration and Prime Minister Margaret Thatcher rigorously followed his precepts.

Right: The front page of the *Wall Street Journal* for Tuesday, October 20, 1987, the day after the Dow Jones Average lost 23%. Other stock exchanges around the world also crashed following the bad news.

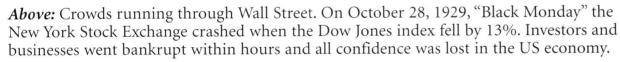

Above: Crowds running through Wall Street. On October 28, 1929, "Black Monday" the New York Stock Exchange crashed when the Dow Jones index fell by 13%. Investors and businesses went bankrupt within hours and all confidence was lost in the US economy.

Left: The ATM was invented by Luther Simjian in 1960 and revolutionized the way account holders get access to their money. No longer was it necessary to have a human teller, a simple numerical pin (personal identification number) was sufficient to withdraw money from an ATM. This machine, which appeared in February 2000, took this a step further by using an iris recognition system.

Right: Organization of the Petroleum Exporting Countries (OPEC) Secretary General Alvaro Silva Calderon at the OPEC HQ in Vienna, March 20, 2003. OPEC was set up in 1960 to protect and guide the interests of oil producing countries. Now with 13 members it is a powerful cartel which fixes world prices for crude oil and the quantities extracted. Member countries have become exceedingly rich on the proceeds of such selective selling.

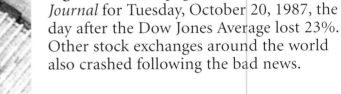

Above: Almost all British coins became obsolete on February 15, 1971 when the UK decimalized its currency.

THE WALL STREET JOURNAL.

Above: Traders at the Chicago Stock Exchange show disbelief and horror on their faces as stocks plummet on Wall Street during the crash of 1987. Many businesses failed in the aftermath and the day quickly became known as "Black Monday"—as did the crash of Monday October 28, 1929.

Below: Hillary Clinton and Dutch princess Margriet seen after their husbands had signed an historic NATO-Russia accord. President Clinton had attended commemorations for the 50th anniversary of the US Marshall Aid Plan which helped war-damaged European countries.

Below: Trader George Soros became notorious when he made billions betting against sterling and in the process forcing the UK to withdraw sterling from the ERM on Black Wednesday. Sterling subsequently fell 15% in value against the Deutschmark.

Below: Official photograph of the heads of state at the Group of Eight (G8) summit meeting held at the French lakeside resort of Evian on Sunday June 1, 2003. (L–R, front row) Mexican President Vicente Fox, Senegalese President Abdoulaye Wade, Nigerian President Olusegun Obasanjo, Egyptian President Hosni Mubarak, French President Jacques Chirac, Algerian President Abdelaziz Bouteflika, South African President Thabo Mbeki, Russian President Vladimir Putin, Indian Prime Minister Atal Bihari Vajpayee; (L–R, 2nd row) UN Secretary General Kofi Annan, Saudi Arabian Crownprince Prince Abdullah Ibn Abdul Aziz Al Saud, Brazilian President Luiz Inacio Lula da Silva, US President George W. Bush, Chinese President Hu Jintao, Swiss President Pascal Couchepin, Canadian Prime Minister Jean Chretien (R); (2nd L–R, back row) President of the World Bank James Wolfensohn, Greek Prime Minister Costas Simitis, Japanese Prime Minister Junichiro Koizumi, British Prime Minister Tony Blair, Italian Prime Minister Silvio Berlusconi and EU Commission President Romano Prodi.

Above: President Bill Clinton waving goodbye from Marine One on the South Lawn of the White House February 14, 1999. He is about to leave for Andrews Air Force Base before going to Mexico. Clinton to meet Mexican President Ernesto Zedillo will hold a summit touching on all US-Mexican issues, in particular the important issues of environment and trade.

Above: During the final leg of his week-long European trip President Bill Clinton addressed the Commeration of the 50th anniversary of the World Trade Organization at the Salle des Assemblee in the Palais des Nations, May 18, 1998, in Geneva, Switzerland. The WTO replaced the General Agreement on Tariffs and Trade (GATT) in 1994 and is supported by 97 member states. Its powers are wider than its predecessor and include agreeing international trading rules and the liberation of international trade.

Left: One of the great success stories of the Internet is Amazon.com which sells books through the world wide web, although it took a long time to turn a profit. Here on June 28, 2000 ,the chairman and CEO Jeff Bezos discusses new features of the company's website during a speech at the PC Expo in New York.

Below: In February 1997 Bill Gates became the worlds richest man. In 1975 age 19 he left Harvard without graduating and co-founded Microsoft Corporation with Paul Allen. Microsoft quickly became dominant in the PC market and its Windows operating system is constantly updated to keep ahead of the opposition.

Below: The Bundesbank is the German central bank that originally controlled the eleven regional banks in the former West Germany, it now oversees all German banks. Its president Hans Tietmeyer retired at the same time as the Deutchmark was replaced by the Euro, January 1, 1999.

Above: Frankfurt, Germany has been the home of the European Central Bank since 1998 when the Euro was officially launched.

Above: In October 1987 Finance ministers and central bank governors from the seven most industrialized countries began a meeting in Palermo, Sicily, to discuss the global impact of a slowdown in US growth. This was dubbed the "End of the Bull Run." Attending the meeting were Chairman of the US Federal Reserve Bank Alan Greenspan (at left), and US Treasury Secretary Paul O'Neill during the Group of Seven finance ministers meeting.

Left: On April 13, 1999 the Chinese Premier Zhu Rongji visited the Nasdaq-Amex Market Site in New York. Frank Zarb chairman and CEO of the National Association of Security Dealers, watches as he signs the guest book.

Above: On January 1, 2002 all the European countries which had elected to join the Euro changed their banknotes and coins into Euros. Vending machines, toll booths, and all types of coin slot machines had to be changed to accommodate the new currency.

Left: The two massive international media giants America Online and Time Warner announced their merger at a New York news conference on January 10, 2000. AOL is one of the major internet providers and Time Warner have extensive interests across a broad spectrum but principally in movies and television. Announced by (AOL) chairman Steve Case (at left) and Time Warner chairman Gerald Levin. The new company is called AOL Time Warner.

The criminal world flourishes in most societies working openly or covertly for its own selfish means. It generates much of its cash from the twilight worlds of gambling, drug running, and prostitution. In some countries such crime is tacitly supported by the governments, who use it as a means to generate foreign currency which they are otherwise unable to acquire. Generally speaking, crime in the twentieth century has got better organized than previously, as technology has helped the criminal to extend his reach. Nowadays with computer crime money can vanish completely while the perpetrator can be sitting at his or her console half a world away. Computer fraud has become one of the biggest problems facing organizations such as Interpol.

Crime has been increasingly glamorized by novels, TV, and movies to the extent that some criminals have acquired quasi hero status. The real life Bonnie and Clyde were a thoroughly ruthless pair of thieves and murderers, but thanks to the film of that name their nastiness has been reduced to a "caper" with no reflection of the truth. This is also true of many named perpetrators whose stories are glossed over and sensationalized in film in virtually every language spoken on the planet. Most familiar crime and criminals are American villains immortalized in the movies. The real Al Capone, responsible for the St Valentine's massacre in Chicago in 1929, made his money and notoriety from racketeering during the Prohibition era. He made money from prostitution, bootlegging, and gambling and got away with it for a long time by bribing local Chicago police to look the other way.

The Prohibition era lasted from the passing of the 18th Amendment which became effective from January 16, 1920, until repealed by the 21st Amendment of 1933.

CRIME

Although promulgated for sound moral reasons (to stop widespread drunkenness) the law actually allowed organized crime to take a grip on America. This started with large scale bootlegging—running alcohol across all the US borders—which made a fortune for those involved but quickly developed into racketeering, prostitution, and gambling. Such vast sums of money were illegally collected that it enabled groups such as the Italian Mafia to establish a stronghold in America.

Since the 1960s some of the most prosperous criminal elements are involved with the drug trade: cocaine from Columbia, heroin from the Golden Triangle in the Far East, hashish from North Africa and the Middle East. Drug money is at the root of much criminal activity and is the target of government agencies in countries all around the world. As well as the major problems of trafficking and selling, the end-users of the drugs need to find money to be able to sustain their dependence on their drugs. The growth of drug culture leads directly to the growth of mugging, burglary, car theft, and other street crime. A significant percentage of all crime is drug-related, and a significant percentage of this is petty crimes of theft.

It is, however, true to say that murder is the crime that most catches the public's attention. There is certainly an element of fear in this: the notorious serial killers such as Geoffrey Dhamer, the Boston Strangler, and the Yorkshire Ripper caused entire cities and neighborhoods to became no-go areas as people (mostly women) became too frightened to venture out alone after dark. The 20th century seemed to have more than its fair share of killers. The world political environment, which saw tens of millions killed in war, famine, state-sponsored purges or genocide, may well have contributed to this. Certainly vicarious Press reporting means that everyone is made more aware of all the bloody incidents that punctuate our lives.

1986
Largest cocaine bust took over 2 tons of powder at West Palm Beach, Florida.

1987
Klaus Barbie, age 73, former Gestapo wartime chief in Lyon, sentenced to life by French court for war crimes.

1990.
Junk bond wizard Michael Milkin faced 98 indictments of fraud and racketeering. Found guilty and sentenced to ten years in jail and $600 million in fines.

1991
Notorious publisher Robert Maxwell drowned at sea. Soon revealed that he fraudulently used millions of pounds of company pension funds.

BCCI Scandal. Bank of Credit & Commerce International. Defrauded billions out of its investors and charged with running corrupt money-laundering.

1994
Carlos the Jackal caught in the Sudan. and handed over to the French. Already tried *in absentia* in France and sentenced to life.

Aldrich Ames,an important C.I.A. official, charged with spying for Soviets who paid him over $2 million. Indicted for treason, he sold critical defense secrets and caused the deaths of at least 11 US agents

1995
Serial killer Frederick West, accused of 12 murders, found hanged in his prison cell on New Years Day.

1998
"Hacker" and "Worm" enter the Internet lexicon. First data crime reported.

Unabomber, Theodore Kaczynski, sentenced to four life terms for sending 16 mail bombs to a variety of targets, killing three and seriously injuring 23.

1999
Two disaffected students go on shooting spree in Columbine High School, killing 15 and themselves.

Dr. Jack Kevorkian convicted of second-degree murder in assisted-suicide case.

Day-trader kills 9 and wounds 13 in two Atlanta brokerage offices before committing suicide.

Jeffrey Archer sentenced to four years for perjury and perverting the course of justice.

2000
Love Bug virus infects 45 million computers.

2001
Former Ku Klux Klansman Thomas E. Blanton convicted of the 1963 murder of four black girls in Birmingham, Alabama.

FBI agent Robert Hanssen is charged with spying for the Soviet Union for 15 years.

2002
Former Serbian president Slobodan Milosevic tried for crimes against humanity.

Tyco executives L. Dennis Kozlowski and Mark Swartz indicted in stock-fraud scheme.

Former ImClone Executive Sam Waksal pleads guilty to charges including fraud and perjury.

Snipers prey upon DC suburbs, killing ten and wounding others. Police arrest two sniper suspects, John Allen Muhammad and John Lee Malvo.

Serial killer Dr Harold Shipman found guilty of killing 15 women patients; suspected of some 150 more.

Former Enron executive Michael Kopper pleads guilty to financial wrongdoing.

2003
Serial killer Robert William Pickton charged with the first-degree murders of 15 women at a preliminary hearing in Port Coquitlam, Canada.

Major Charles Ingram, charged with fraud for cheating his way to the top prize on *Who Wants To Be A Millionaire?* using an accomplices coded coughs.

The heads of the five New York Mafia families for the first time simultaneously behind bars.

Above: James R. Hoffa, vice president of the Teamsters Union, testifying before the Senate Rackets Committee in Washington, DC. on August 20, 1957. Following release from prison in 1975 he went missing, presumed murdered. His body has never been found.

Above: Klaus Barbie, 73, Gestapo wartime chief in Lyon, was sentenced to life by a French court in July 1987 for war crimes. Beate Klarsfeld, wife of Serge Klarsfeld president of the association of French Jewish Deportees' Children, who tracked Barbie down, inspects the Izieu memorial, an exhibition dedicated to the long search.

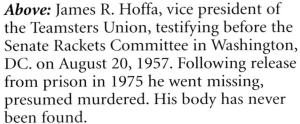

Above: A collection of knives used by the serial killer Andrei Chikatilo. The former teacher was found guilty of cannibalism and fifty-two murders in the Rostov region of Russia between 1978 and 1990, although there were probably more victims. During his six-month trial he was kept in a steel cage. Sentenced to death, he was executed in 1994.

Above: New York Gambino Mafia family boss John Gotti during a break in his trial for racketeering in January 1990. The "Teflon Don" walked away from three trials but was finally convicted in April 1992 on multiple charges that included five murders. He died from cancer after serving ten years in jail in Missouri.

Above: The remains of disgraced peer Lord Brocket's exotic car collection—three Ferraris, two Maseratis and a pile of spares from other wrecked classics—were sold by his creditors, after being discovered dismantled in a London garage. Lord Brocket was jailed for five years for a £4.5 million insurance fraud, He had forced three of his estate workers to help him destroy the cars which he claimed had been stolen.

Below: The Unabomber—Harvard graduate, doctor of mathematics, and hermit, Theodore Kaczynski—was sentenced to four life terms on May 4, 1998. He targeted people who represented manipulative industries and fields that helped isolate people from nature and one another.

Above: Gloucester builder Frederick West was accused of 12 murders but escaped justice by hanging himself in his prison cell. However his wife and accomplice Rosemary West was accused and sentenced for the murders of 10 people including those of her daughter, Heather, 16, and eight-year-old step-daughter Charmaine.

Above: Twenty-three French police officers of a highway patrol unit near the Spanish border in court April 20, 1998, in Perpignan, southwestern France. They were charged with a series of offenses, including corruption, theft, and fraud. The prosecution alleged that the unit was particularly efficient in stopping law-breaking motorists between 1993 and 1996, but drivers then found they would escape getting a ticket if they showed their "generosity" to the officer.

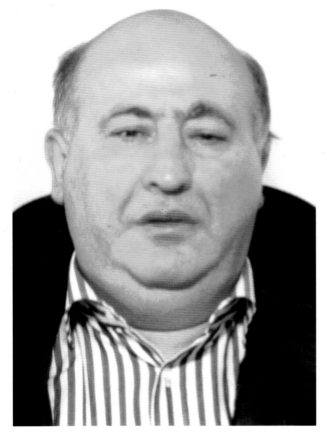

Above: On the run since 1993, mafia boss Giuseppe Piromalli, was one of Italy's most wanted fugitives. He was finally arrested March 10, 1999, in an apparently abandoned building in Gioia Tauro, Southern Italy. The head of the Gioia Tauro clan was sentenced to life imprisonment for two murders. Police said 54-year-old Piromalli was seized in his own fiefdom in a hideout which had a security system worthy of a James Bond film.

Above: Police escort Anatoly Onopriyenko to the courtroom in Jitomir in March 1999 at the end of his four-month trial. The Ukrainian court convicted the self-confessed serial killer on 52 murder charges and sentenced him to death.

Above: Police officers gather in front of Columbine High School, in Littleton, CO, on March 4, 1999, before searching the building to insure that it was secure following a shooting spree by two masked teenagers. 15 students were killed when two gunmen opened fire on their fellow students inside the school building, before turning their weapons on themselves.

Above: Assisted suicide advocate Dr. Jack Kevorkian leaves the court with his sister, Flora Holzheimer, after he was convicted of second-degree murder in Oakland County Circuit Court on March 26, 1999, in Pontiac, Michigan.

Above: Antonio Barea, Andrew Jalassola, and Joe Lowrey were part of a gang of international fraudsters who nearly duped St Paul's Cathedral, London, out of £100 million. The gang posed as Hollywood film producers and asked St Paul's to give them the money to put in a United States Treasury-linked investment scheme, which would make them another £50 million—enough to renovate the cathedral's dome. The plot was foiled after a tip-off to police who sent in undercover agents posing as financiers. Italian Barea, 28, pleaded guilty to conspiracy to defraud St Paul's and was sentenced to six months—although he was immediately released as he had served that time in custody. The two other men, American Lowrey, 67, and Andrew Jalassola, 32, from Finland, were arrested and charged in June 1999, but when bailed by the courts absconded to West Palm Beach, Florida, where they cannot be extradited.

Above: Rogue trader Nick Leeson, who brought down Barings Bank, being escorted back to a news conference at London's Heathrow airport the day after he was released from a Singapore jail on July 4, 1999.

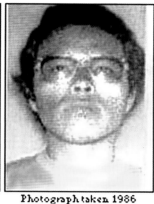

Photograph taken 1980's   Photograph taken 1986   Photograph taken 1986   Photograph taken 1989

Photograph taken 1993   Photograph taken 1996   Photograph taken 1998   Photograph taken 1998

Above: These FBI photos show the different faces of a suspected serial killer and one of America's "Ten Most Wanted," Rafael Resendez-Ramirez. Suspected of being the "Railroad Killer" Ramirez was linked to eight murders in Kentucky, Texas and in Illinois. The FBI announced that he surrendered to authorities in Texas on July 13, 1999. He is not to be confused with another serial killer, the "Nightstalker"— Richard Ramirez—who has been on death row in St. Quentin since 1995.

Right: Serial killer, Javed Iqbal arriving in court under police custody in Lahore, Pakistan. Iqbal, 38, was convicted of murdering 100 children and sentenced to death by a Pakistani high court but was found dead in his high-security cell after he commited suicide on October 10, 2001.

Above: Reggie Kray's horse-drawn hearse drives through East London while people line the streets along the route to St. Matthew's Church in Bethnal Green, Tuesday October 11, 2000. Kray, who died of cancer, was one of Britain's most feared gangsters and held a mafia-like grip on London's East End during the 1960s. Reggie Kray and his twin brother Ronnie were convicted of murder and sentenced to life in prison in 1969.

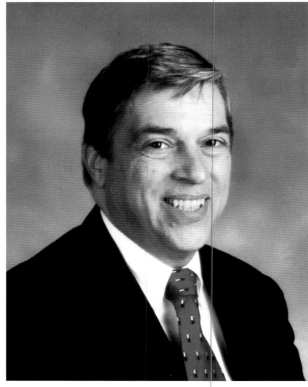

Above: Official FBI photo of Robert Philip Hanssen accused of spying for Russia for 15 years. In May 2001 Hanssen was offered a deal to plead guilty to espionage and brief the government on the full extent of his actions in exchange for a life sentence.

Above: Jefferson County, Alabama, Sheriff's Department photo released May 17, 2000, of Thomas E. Blanton, Jr. In 1963 Birmingham's Baptist Church was the target of a racist bomb which killed four African-American girls. Blanton, a former Ku Klux Klan member, was found guilty of murder on four counts and sentenced to four consecutive life terms in May 2001.

Left: Fugitive Mafia boss Vincenzo Virga was arrested by Italian police on February 21, 2001. Virga was one of the ten most wanted criminals in Italy and one of the most trusted accolytes of the Mafia supreme boss, Bernardo Provenzano.

Right: Lord Jeffrey Archer arriving at the Theatre Royal in Lincoln, March 2002. Responding to criticism from local people about Archer's lenient treatment, the head of the Prison Service, Martin Narey said that Lord Archer was being treated "no differently" to any other prisoner while being allowed out of jail to work at a theater. Archer worked behind the scenes while on day release from his open prison. The disgraced peer, who was given a four-year sentence for perjury and perverting the course of justice, was employed five days a week at the Theatre Royal in Lincoln. He was paid for his work and returned every night to the North Sea Camp prison near Boston, Lincolnshire.

Above: WorldCom headquarters in Clinton, Mississippi as it looked on June 26, 2002, the day after the company announced the planned layoff of 17,000 workers. The company collapsed as investigations into financial mishandling meant that charges were being brought in one of the largest fraud cases ever filed in US history.

Right: Serial killer Dr Harold Shipman was found guilty at Preston Crown Court in January 2000 of the murders of 15 of his patients in Hyde, Greater Manchester. Due to the suspicion that there were more victims a later inquiry was held in July 2002 by High Court judge Dame Janet Smith. This found that Shipman murdered 215 of his mainly elderly women patients as well as a probable further 45 victims. This advertisement was published in two national and three local papers in an attempt to trace the relatives of more than 80 former patients of Dr Harold Shipman.

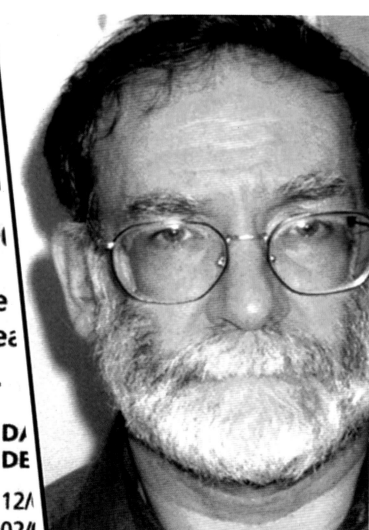

Above: Former WorldCom chief financial officer Scott Sullivan being led out of the Federal Building in New York by FBI agents after being arrested in August 2002 on charges stemming from the collapse of WorldCom. Sullivan is accused of overseeing a scheme to conceal $3.8 billion in company expenses and was indicted August 28, 2002, on securities fraud and other charges after an apparent breakdown in plea negotiations. The indictment also names a new defendant, Buford Yates Jr., the former director of general accounting at WorldCom.

Left: Former Enron executive Michael Kopper outside the Federal Courts Building in Houston, Texas, in August 2002. Kopper plead guilty to financial wrongdoing and agreed to surrender $12 million in the first criminal case against a company official. Kopper, a former director in Enron's global financial unit, pleaded guilty to single counts of conspiracy to commit wire fraud and conspiracy to commit money laundering.

Below: Another fraud, another accountant. Former ImClone Executive Sam Waksal pleaded guilty to charges including fraud and perjury in October 2002.

Above: Former Tyco CEO Dennis Kozlowski leaving the Manhattan Criminal Court September 19, 2001, after his bail hearing. Kozlowski and former chief finance officer Mark Swartz were indicted the week before on state charges of "stealing more than $170 million from Tyco and obtaining more than $430 million by fraud in the sale of securities." The accused were allowed by a judge to post bail while awaiting charges of using the firm as a "criminal enterprise." The prosecution said it may challenge the source of the bail funds to be used by the former Tyco executives. If convicted, Kozlowski and Swartz face up to 25 years in prison on each count of corruption and larceny charges as well as 30 years in prison on conspiracy charges.

Above: Sniper suspect, John Allen Muhammad is led into court prior to a hearing at the Prince William County Court in Manassas, Va., Monday, June 30, 2003. The judge upheld the constitutionality of the state's anti terrorism ordinance as it applied to the case.

Above: Benedetto Marciante, the fugitive Mafia boss who turned himself in to police on Thursday, November 14, 2002, prompted by Pope John Paul II's speech to the Italian Parliament on Christian values which was broadcast live around the country. Marciante, 50, native of Sicily, has been sentenced to 30 years in prison for murder and seven years for association with the Mafia. He surrendered to police in Rome where he was in hiding, his lawyer, Roberto Tricoli, said: "The Pope's words moved him so much, he immediately turned himself in."

Left: This courtroom drawing shows Robert William Pickton during a preliminary hearing in Port Coquitlam, 35km (22 miles) east of Vancouver, January 13, 2003. The mystery behind what happened to dozens of women who disappeared over a 25-year period from Vancouver may finally start to unravel at the hearing for Pickton, Canada's worst accused serial killer. Pickton, a 53-year-old suburban pig farmer, is charged with the first-degree murders of 15 of the women who vanished from Vancouver's seedy Downtown Eastside. Pickton's alleged victims, aged 22 to 46, were mainly prostitutes or drug addicts.

Above: Major Charles Ingram, who cheated his way to the top prize on the TV program Who Wants To Be A Millionaire? Ingram used an accomplice's coded coughs to reach the quiz show jackpot.

Left: Vietnam's most notorious gangster Truong Van Cam, aged 55, also known as, Nam Cam, is taken from the Ho Chi Minh City courthouse surrounded by police after hearing his sentence of death Thursday, June 5, 2003. Nam Cam was at the center of Vietnam's biggest organized crime case involving 155 defendants facing charges linked to alleged corruption in the highest levels of the Communist Party.

Above: A policewoman stands next to a priceless painting by 16th century artist Parmigianino, in Genoa June 11, 2003. The painting was stolen from a monastery in northwest Italy almost a decade ago. It has been recovered by Italian art sleuths, police said. The oil on wood was found by Genoa art police in a villa under construction near Italy's border with France, police said.

Above: Andrew Luster is escorted by law enforcement officers after his arrival from Mexico at Los Angeles International Airport, Thursday, June 19, 2003. The FBI put cosmetics heir Luster aboard a plane in Mexico and flew him back to California on Thursday, five months after he was convicted in absentia of drugging and raping three women.

Above: Policemen set fire on confiscated heroin in Shenzhen in southeast China. Over 300lb of drugs seized in the past year by Shenzhen Customs were burned in public as an anti-drugs education measure on June 26, 2003— International Anti Drug Day—with another four tons of drugs melted at a local garbage disposal center. Shenzhen is one of the most important transfer stations of drug traffic in China.

Above: Thai police guard the six tonnes of illegal drugs including 61 million tablets of methamphetamine (pink tablets pictured), 114,070 tablets of ecstasy, and 650lb of heroin on Thursday, June 26, 2003, near Bangkok. The drugs were worth an estimated street value of 305 million euros.

Above Right: Police photograph of money recovered from the Security Express Robbery. Britain's biggest investigation into police corruption finally smashed the fantastic lifestyles of a closely-knit gang of "supercops" who became a law unto themselves and stole thousands of pounds.

Right: Three unidentified Chinese nationals are arrested in South Africa's largest drug bust by members of the Scorpions Investigative Unit at a house in the northern suburbs of Johannesburg, South Africa, Thursday July 3, 2003. The drugs, with a street value of approximately $100 million, were confiscated and a total of seven people arrested at various locations north of Johannesburg, with the Chinese suspects being linked to the notorious Chinese Triads.

The story of the 20th century seems to be a story of war. No other period of history can compare in terms of numbers killed. Even that ultimate killing machine, the Mongol horde of Temujin, self-styled Genghis Khan (Universal Ruler), cannot be compared to the effects of the two world wars. A combination of nationalism, dictatorships, genocidal political systems, and technology allowed humans to perform miracles in terms of the numbers of people they could kill. The machine gun seemed to be the ultimate killing weapon to those in the trenches in 1915, but the century was able to provide much worse than that: poison gas, tanks, bombing from aircraft, nuclear weapons, rockets and cruise missiles, "Star Wars"—the development of killing technology paid a seemingly neverending tribute to humankind's ability to kill their fellows.

The century started with the great colonial power of Britain at war in South Africa, fighting the Boers. In 1904 Russia and Japan came to blows in a war that took place mainly in Korea and Manchuria—two countries that would see little peace for the next century. These wars were overshadowed by conflict that grew from the troubled Balkans. Conquered by the Turks in the 14th and 15th centuries, fought over by the Austro-Hungarian Empire, the peoples of the Balkans were throwing off their shackles and fighting for their freedom. The emnities created by half a millennium of oppression, as well as the diverse ethnicity and religion of the peoples of the Balkans, would lead the world into war. On June 28, 1914, Gavrilo Princip—a Bosnian-born Serb member of a gang dedicated to the independence of the south slavs of the Austro-Hungarian Empire—assassinated the empire's crown prince, Franz Ferdinand. Austria attacked Serbia and the web of European treaties, economic and political rivalries propelled the world into a conflict that all who took part thought was the war to end all wars. Fought

WAR

mainly in Europe, the Middle East, Africa, and at sea, between the Central Powers (Austria-Hungary, Germany, Bulgaria, and Turkey) and the Allies (Britain, France, Russia, Belgium, Serbia, Greece, Romania, Montenegro, Portugal, Italy, Japan, and, latterly, the United States), some 10 million combatants would be killed, 20 million wounded, and untold numbers of civilians dispossessed of homes, households, and livelihoods.

The historian can see that the Armistice of November 11, 1918—and the peace conferences that followed it—was more like a half-time whistle than anything else. But that hypothesis downplays the culpability of Adolf Hitler and the Nazi party in causing the next conflict. From the moment they gained power in Germany in 1933, the views

and agendas of the Nazis were always going to lead to war—war against the East, and a political system—Communism—totally antithetic to their own; and war against the free world.

As everyone knows, the Nazis and their allies, the Japanese, lost to a combination of the old world superpower, the British Empire, and the two new ones, the United States and the Soviet Union. But the first use of atomic weapons to end the fight in the Pacific changed the face of global war. While the world recovered from a conflict that had caused over 50 million deaths, a new type of war took place between the superpowers—the Cold War. With both sides walking a tightrope that saw armageddon a possibility, the Cold War rarely became hot. When it did, it led to bloody wars by proxy: Korea, Vietnam, Arab versus Israeli. The eventual fall of Communism saw the United States become the most powerful nation on earth—but this in itself has not put paid to wars, as events in the Somalia, Afghanistan, and the Gulf have proved.

---

of State of Israel after British mandate ends and the Arabs attack.

1948–60
Malaya Confrontation as Communists try to take over.

1948–2003
Kashmir war between India and Pakistan follows partition of India. Outbreaks of violence continue through century, including second Indo-Pakistan war of 1965.

1950–53
Korean war follows North Korean invasion of the south. China joins in on Nov. 26.

1954–62
French-Algerian war. Rebellion against French rule begins Oct. 31.

1956
Suez Crisis—British and French forces seize Suez, Oct 31. Second Arab-Israeli war in Sinai. Soviets invade Hungary.

1962
Cuban missile crisis after Russians set up missile sites.

1964–73
Vietnam war between south (with US asistance) and Communist north.

1967
Third Arab-Israeli war—the Six-Day War—starts with an Israeli preemptive strike.

1967–70
Nigeria-Biafra civil war.

1968
Soviets invade Czechoslovia.
Tet offensive in Vietnam.

1971
Pakistan-Bangladesh civil war leads to third Indo-Pakistan War.

1973
Fourth Arab-Israeli war—called Yom Kippur war after Arab attack.

1974–91
Ethiopian civil war following deposing of Emperor Haile Selassie.

1975–2002
Angolan civil war follows on from Angolan war of indepoendence from Portugal.

1976–98
Indonesia-East Timor civil war.

1979–88
Soviet Union invades Afghanistan. The war—Russia's Vietnam—will involve huge numbers of Russian troops.

1980–88
Iran-Iraq war—which will see over a million casualties—starts when Saddam Hussein invades (Sept. 22).

1982
Falklands War follows Argentine invasion of Apr. 2 British Task Force sails and retakes islands by June 14.

1991
First Gulf War takes place following Saddam Hussein's invasion of Kuwait. Large coalition against Iraq to liberates the country but does not depose Saddam.

1990–96
Balkan civil wars follow the break up of Yugoslavia and fall of Communism.

1992–99
Algerian civil war

1994–
Russians attack Chechen guerillas in breakaway republic of Chechnya.

1994
Rwanda's civil war continues genocidal conflict betwen Hutus and Tutsis.

1999
Kosovo's liberation war—NATO vs Serbia .

2001
Following Al-Queda's Twin Towers atrocity US-led coalition attacks Afghanistan and Taliban regime hiding Osama Bin Laden.

2003
Second Gulf War sees Saddam Hussein's regime in Iraq deposed by a coalition of western powers (US, UK, Australia) in continued war against terrorism.

Left: British soldiers in trenches in modern-day Iraq, August 1, 1915. The Indian Expeditionary Force advanced up the River Tigris towards Baghdad— then part of Turkish Mesopotamia—in summer and Autumn 1915. The force was held at Ctesiphon and surrounded at Kut from December 7. Besieged by greater Turkish forces, the 6th Indian Division finally surrendered on April 30.

Below: Scenes outside Buckingham Palace on Armistice Day, November 11, 1918, when the royal family appeared on the balcony to celebrate the end of the war with servicemen and civilians.

Above: Under British guard, German prisoners of war mend the road and clear rubble in the northern French town of Bethune, December 1918. Germany paid dearly for losing the war—as well as reparations and occupation, German troops were put to work clearing the detritus of war.

Right: The charismatic T. E. Lawrence—Lawrence of Arabia—seen astride a motorcycle, on March 26, 1927. He would die in a motorcycle accident eight years later, when he crashed his Brough Superior near Wareham, Dorset. A lieutenant colonel in the war, he reenlisted afterward using assumed names to serve as J. H. Ross in the Royal Air Force and T. E. Shaw in the Royal Amoured Corps. Conspiracy theorists have argued that his death was no accident but planned by the British intelligence service to stop Lawrence from siding with Mosley and his Blackshirts.

Left: The Blitz of London—a destroyed building burns following a German bombing raid on September 9, 1940. Following the fall of France in summer 1940, when only Britain and its Empire stood against Hitler, the German air force tried to pound the British into submission preparatory to an invasion. But when this failed, from September the attacks were made on British cities. The effects on civilian morale were significant but transitory: half the non-military casualties of the war came in this period as 80,000 died in the attacks. Over half the raids were on London, which lost over a million homes to bombing.

Below: A Luftwaffe Junkers Ju 52 transport aircraft of XI Air Corps is unloaded by *Fallschirmjäger* (paratroopers) taking part in the successful airborne invasion of the Greek island of Crete (Operation "*Merkur*"). The battle had very different effects on the staff of each side. Hitler, horrified by the losses incurred by the Germans, did not use *Fallschirmjäger* again in a major airdrop. The Allies, on the other hand, redoubled their training and would use significant numbers of paratroops in the invasion of Normandy, at Arnhem, and the Rhine crossing.

WAR

Left: US battleship *Arizona* (BB 39) is hit during the Japanese December 7 attack on Pearl Harbor. A strategic coup designed to destroy the United States' major naval assets in one preemptive strike, the Japanese sneak attack took place when the US carriers were out of port. While the losses were major—18 warships including eight battleships, 187 aircraft and nearly 2,500 men—it was the carriers that would win the Pacific War.

Right: German mountain troops from the 1st Gebirgsjäger Division in snow-camouflaged overalls during their climb to the summit of Mount Elbrus in the Caucasus on August 14, 1942. Captain Grod and his men climbed the 5,000m mountain in a typical early war propaganda event: within six months, however, the Germans were on the retreat and by mid-February 1943 Soviet forces were able to stage their own propaganda coup as the hammer and sickle flag was planted once more on the summit of Elbrus.

Left: Another major propaganda exercise, this photograph shows the damage inflicted on the Eder dam in Germany by the RAF's No. 617 Squadron, the "Dambusters." Using the remarkable bouncing bombs, designed by Barnes Wallis, the night attack on May 16, 1943, saw 19 Lancaster aircraft commanded by Wing Commander Guy Gibson, who won the Victoria Cross for his leadership, breach the Mohne and Eder dams in the Ruhr. Seven aircraft were shot down.

Below: The most important battle on the Western Front took place on June 6, 1944 when the Allies landed in Normandy. Having secured their foothold on the Continent of Europe in the face of stiff opposition, they would liberate Northwestern Europe and end the Nazi regime within 10 months.

WAR

Above: The death toll in opposed amphibious landings is always high. This photograph of a Normandy beach could have been taken on the coast of northwest Africa during Operation "Torch," on the beaches of Sicily, Italy, Southern France or any of the Pacific Islands assaulted by the Allies during the war.

Left: Breakout from Normandy! Spearheaded by troops of General George Patton's Third Army at Avranches, Operation "Cobra" dislodged the German defenders and started a rout that would end in their decimation in the Falaise Pocket.

Left: The war has reached its final months. In January 1945, two German soldiers—although it's hard to consider anyone this young a soldier—are captured by US troops. To defend his "Thousand-Year Reich," Hitler would call upon old and young in a senseless scorched earth policy.

Below: Views of the results of American bombing of Yokohama, south of Tokyo. The US 20th Air Force, using the mightiest World War II bomber, the B-29 Superfortress, devastated the Japanese mainland in a series of incendiary attacks from the Marianas Islands which were captured in summer 1944.

WAR

Left: Into the Reich! Soldiers of the 39th Infantry Regiment (US 9th Division) make their way through the anti-tank "dragon's teeth" during their advance through the Siegfried Line into Germany. The Siegfried Line was a series of fortifications running for hundreds of miles along Germany's western border, constructed in the 1930s.

Below: Bodies discovered by Allied troops lying in a mass grave at Belsen concentration camp, near Hamburg, Germany, towards the end of the Second World War. Bergen-Belsen was liberated by British troops on April 15, 1945. The camps had been built as soon as the Nazis came to power, and had been used for genocide from the early war years. The resulting Holocaust killed at least six million people—mainly European Jews—although the total could well have been double that figure.

Above: The late 1940s was the period when the Cold War divide between Communist and Free World took shape. In Europe, the Berlin Blockade would last from April 1948 to May 1949, the Communists took over in Czechoslovakia, and fighting between Communists and government troops took place in Greece. In China, Communists took Peking in 1949 forcing Nationalist leader Chiang Kai-shek to retreat to Formosa. In 1950 the North Korean War Communists attacked the south, driving past the 38th parallel. The UN immediately pledged direct military aid. Here, North Korean prisoners kneel as they wait for questioning.

Above Right: US forces reached Korea at the end of June 1950, and the UN forces followed, British troops arriving in late August. By then most of South Korea was in Communist hands, with UN troops confined in a small area around Pusan. General Douglas MacArthur's brilliant amphibious assault at Inchon on September 16 and a breakout from Pusan pushed the Koreans back to the Chinese border. This led to the entry of China into the war which would drag on until July 26, 1953. This photo shows US infantry moving past civilians, caught in the fighting.

Left: The mushroom cloud above Hiroshima, August 6, 1945, after B-29 Superfortress *Enola Gay* ushered in the atomic age.

Right: The two sides—the South Korean on the left guards two North Koreans captured in the fighting.

WAR

Left: In mid-June 1956 British and French troops left the Suez Canal Zone leaving the President of Egypt, Abdel Nasser, free to nationalize the company running it. In Operation "Musketeer" British and French forces retook the canal. An Israeli offensive took place in Sinai at the same time—although any link between the Anglo-French and Israeli attacks was strongly denied. Unsurprisingly, the Egyptian forces were routed. Here, British Paras show off a captured Russian-built Su-100 tank destroyer at Port Said.

Left: The Anglo-French forces attacked both from the sea and the air, quickly capturing their objectives—including El Gamel airfield.

Right: The Communist takeover of Cuba in 1958 led to a thorn in the side of the United States that still exists. In 1960 Castro nationalized US property; the US retaliated by breaking off diplomatic relations and sponsoring the abortive April invasion of the island by Cuban exiles— the Bay of Pigs fiasco. In 1961 US president John F Kennedy declared an embargo on Cuban goods (after, it is said, he had ensured a good supply of his favorite cigars). The next year Russian missiles were emplaced on the island leading to an explosive situation relieved only when USSR President Krushchev ordered the dismantling of the sites.

Above: In the immediate postwar period fighting in what had been French Indo-China led to the French withdrawal of troops in 1954–56, the recognition of Laos and Cambodia as independent countries, and the division of Vietnam at the 17th parallel. As the French started to leave, so American military advisers moved in to help the Republic of South Vietnam. By 1961 the Americans had promised to increase the number of "advisers" to 16,000. The "Americanization" of the war grew in pace from then on—by 1966 there will be 400,000 US troops involved. This photograph, dated March 1963, shows Vietnamese paratroopers jumping from US Air Force C-123 transports during Operation Phi Hoa II against the Viet Cong.

Right: A US Marine guards a Viet Cong prisoner as they walk to the collection point October 10, 1965.

WAR

Left: A female Vietcong soldier in action with an RPG-7 anti-tank rocket launcher during fighting as part of the Tet offensive launched in spring 1968. The US forces—now up to 540,000—beat off the attack, but public pressure against American involvement in Southeast Asia is mounting and by the end of 1970 the figure is closer to 270,000.

Below: Prague residents throw stones at Soviet tanks entering their city, during confrontations between demonstrators and the Warsaw Pact troops and tanks, August 21, 1968. The Soviets invaded Czechoslovakia to crush the liberal regime of Eduard Dubcek.

Above: Israeli soldiers atop a US-made Super-Sherman tank on Syria's Golan Heights, a week after the beginning of the Yom Kippur War, October 13, 1973. On October 6, 1973, the Jewish holiday of Yom Kippur, the Arab states launched a brilliant two-pronged assault on Israel, that did much to restore pride lost in earlier wars, particularly Israel's preemptive 1967 strike. Egyptian forces stuck eastward across the Suez Canal and pushed Israelis back, while Syrians advanced from the north and had broken through the Israeli lines on the Golan Heights. It took ten days of hard fighting for the Israelis to regain the initiative. When they did, they poured across the canal, cutting off the Egyptian Third Army: it was only a UN ceasefire that stopped the war.

Right: An Egyptian prisoner-of-war sitting in front of victorious Israeli soldiers flashing V-signs after they established a salient on the West Bank of the Suez canal.

Above: This April 30, 1975, photograph shows a Northern Vietnamese T-54/T-55 tank driving through the main gate of the South Vietnamese presidential palace as Saigon fell into the hands of communist troops. US troops had left in March 1973; April 30 saw South Vietnam surrender to the north and the evacuation of the US embassy by helicopter.

Right: On April 2, 1982, Argentina invaded and seized the Falkland Islands. A British task force sailed to the South Atlantic and landed troops on May 21. Less than three weeks later, on June 14, Argentine forces on the island surrender. The fighting has been fierce at times. This photograph shows survivors of the fleet auxiliary *Sir Galahad* coming ashore in life rafts at San Carlos Bay. Struck by bombs, in the background the supply ship blazes.

Left: British forces in the Falklands were a long way from home with only the air cover that could be provided by the Harriers and Sea Harriers flying off *Hermes* and *Invincible*. They performed brilliantly but could not stop Argentine air forces from knocking out a number of vessels—including HMS *Antelope*. This Type 21 frigate exploded in San Carlos Bay as bomb disposal experts tried to defuse one of three bombs that had hit the vessel.

Below: In 1990 Saddam Hussein invaded Kuwait and a coalition was formed to ensure he withdrew his forces. The Allied air assault against Iraqi forces started on January 16/17 once the UN deadline for Iraqi troop removal ran out. Here British Warrior infantry fighting vehicles and other equipment waits on the dockside at Bremerhaven before shipment to the Gulf

WAR

Above: British forces practice with live ammunition before Operation "Desert Storm" starts the land war on February 24. The war lasts until a formal ceasefire on March 3 by which time Iraqi forces have been obliterated.

Below: Allied air assets attacked the Iraqi military and state infrastructure once they had achieved air supremacy. Here Tornado fighters patrol.

WAR

Left: On the US Air Force's inventory since the mid-1950s, the Boeing B-52 Stratofortress is one of the most successful bomber designs. Gulf War missions by B-52s were undertaken from the continental US as well as the UK. This B-52G was photographed flying into RAF Fairford after a mission to the Gulf.

Right: The breakup of the old Yugoslavia saw the lid taken off the Balkan pressure cooker. Ethnic cleansing, genocide, and murder became commonplace. This photograph dated February 11, 1999, shows ethnic Albanians carrying coffins of massacre victims—there were 45 in total—wrapped in Albanian flags up a hill overlooking Racak, in southern Kosovo.

Below Left: An Egyptian mine-clearing tank launches grenades to explode mines during a training exercise in the Saudi desert during the Gulf War.

Below Right: An Albanian man clears soil from 64 graves being prepared for a mass funeral. Just above the village of Bela Crkva, the scene of several massacres of men, women, and children by Serbian forces, just after NATO air strikes began.

Left: A Greek soldier serving with the NATO mission Operation "Essential Harvest" in Macedonia guards a weapons' collection in a military camp in Krilovak, Macedonia, 95 km southeast of Skopje, Friday, September 14, 2001. NATO forces announced that at the end of the second phase of their Operational "Essential Harvest" 2.276 miscellaneous weapons, parts and ancillaries from Albanian rebels were collected

Below: The result of the 9/11 atrocity was a US attack on Al-Queda forces in Afghanistan—and the Taliban government that housed them. Commercial trucks drive by Northern Alliance fighters on November 24, 2001, after being stranded for more than a week behind Taliban positions some 25 km southwest of Kabul. Following three days of heavy fightings and hours of negotiations the Taliban withdrew from their positions leaving behind their heavy artillery and six tanks.

Above: This US Navy phototograph, dated March 17, 2003, shows a US Navy F-14A Tomcat assigned to the "Black Knights"— Squadron VF-154—loaded with AIM-54C Phoenix and AIM-9 Sidewinder missiles, launching from the flight deck of USS *Kitty Hawk* (CV63), 14 March 2003 in the Persian Gulf.

Right: A Royal Navy Tomahawk missile launched at a target in Iraq, seen through the periscope of the firing submarine.

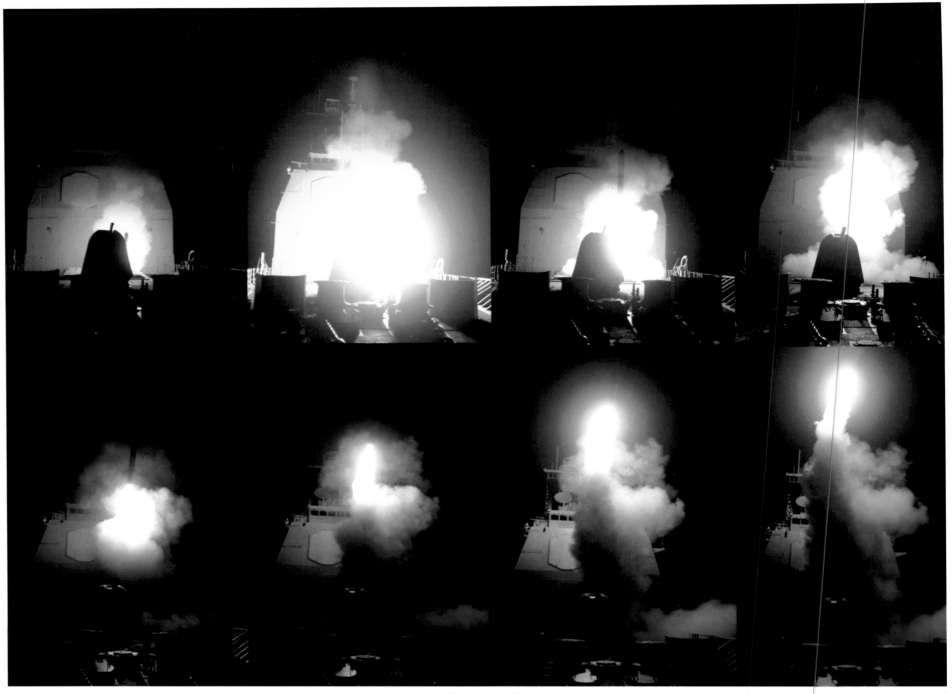

Above: The launch of a Tomahawk cruise missile from the cruiser USS *Shiloh*, March 21, 2003, in Gulf waters. US Defense Secretary Donald Rumsfeld said the air war on Iraq began with a massive US-led air raid on the Iraqi capital Baghdad.

Far Right: Smoke billows from a building in Saddam Hussein's presidential palace complex hit during a US-led air raid on Baghdad, March 23, 2003.

Right: The Royal Scots Dragoon Guards, part of 7 Armoured Brigade, move from Kuwait to Iraq, March 22, 2003.

P olitics is the work of nations and its machinations cause more defining moments than in any other sphere. Politics shape nations—changes to the world map come about through forces—such as war—which are created by politics. The actions of one successful politician can alter history—Adolf Hitler, Stalin, Mao Zedong to name but three. Politics is a complicated and Machiavellian pursuit: conviction politicians can bring about changes in their own countries as well as others, for both good and evil. An inspirational leader such as Nelson Mandela can exert his influence for peace and harmony where the cause seemed hopelessly lost, as Mandela did in South Africa.

Politics has always been a dirty business and few centuries can match the twentieth century for dirty politics. Two world wars and numerous bloody conflicts scarred the

century. In every single year of the century there was at least one country at war with another. Not all wars are international, many of the bloodiest are internal —civil wars such as those in the Balkans, Somalia, Nigeria, Ireland, India, Sri Lanka, and Pakistan as well as many others scarred their nation's psyche.

The repercussions of war are defined in the treaties and agreements made when the dust has settled. Usually one side forces a settlement on the other. In the 1919 Treaty of Versailles drawn up in Paris, the Allies imposed harsh conditions on Germany The Treaty contained 434 articles which deprived Germany of her overseas colonies, conceded German land to Poland, demilitarized the Rhineland, and strictly limited Germany's armed forces as well as imposing massive financial reparations. These punitive measures inevitably caused burning German resentment which in turn led to the rise of nationalism and cleared the path for Adolf Hitler to rise to prominence.

The major political change of the 20th century was the breakup of the British Empire

POLITICAL CHANGE

and replacement of Britain as the dominant force in the world. Some of the elements of empire made the break peacefully—Australia, South Africa, and Canada—others, such as India or Ireland—fought for independence. And, of course, it was not just the British Empire that broke up. By and large the breakup of the empires of the colonial powers was amicable but the results were much more hostile. As the old colonies won their much wanted independence, all too often emerging rival factions led to internal problems. None more so than in India which erupted into turmoil and sectioned into Pakistan, and Bangladesh (formerly East Pakistan), Burma (now the Union of Myanmar), India, and Ceylon (now Sri Lanka).

The other major collapse of empire was that of the Soviet Union. One of the two great

superpowers—the other being the United States—the Soviet Union dominated much of Eastern Europe all the way across the Urals to the Bering Sea and China in the east, to the Caspian and Black Seas in the south. The Cold War between essentially, east and west, brought fear and the very real possibility of nuclear war. Then, while seemingly indestructible and all powerful, the "Iron Curtain" collapsed in 1989, most visibly in Berlin, and virtually overnight the USSR disappeared. In its place emerged a disparate mixture of countries and alliances and Russia shrivelled back to its more or less historic boundaries.

A political vacuum never remains empty for long, other elements invade quickly and occupy the space. The latest empire belongs to the United States of America that uses economic muscle to enforce its will rather than the traditional gunship and bayonet. How this empire will manifest itself only time will tell.

Right: Members of the Chinese regular army during the Chinese Revolution. On October 10, 1911, Sun Yat-Sen the founder and leader of the nationalist revolutionary Kuomintang party organized a revolt that overthrew the ruling Manchu dynasty. Sun was in America when the Chinese Revolution erupted but he returned to China to be hailed in Nanking as President of the United Provinces of China in 1911. This made him nominal leader of the provisional republican government but rival Chinese warlords would not bow to his rule and he only effectively controlled the area around Canton.

Below: Czar Nicholas II with his wife Czarina Alexandra Feodorovna, the Czarevitch (2nd from right) and his four daughters, the Grand Duchesses. Eighty years after Russia's last czar and his family were executed, President Boris Yeltsin planned for their proper burial as a dignified way to close a bloody chapter in Russia's turbulent history. The imperial family's much-disputed bones were placed in small wooden coffins on July 15, 1998 and readied for a state burial alongside their royal ancestors. According to official papers made public for the first time in the year 2000, King George VI intervened personally to secure British citizenship for relatives of the murdered Russian Czar Nicholas II.

Right: A poster issued by members of Sinn Fein proclaiming the creation of an Irish Republic. The rebellion in Dublin, which began on April 24, 1916 claimed the lives of 794 civilians and 521 soldiers and police.

POBLACHT NA H EIREANN

THE PROVISIONAL GOVERNMENT

OF THE

IRISH REPUBLIC

TO THE PEOPLE OF IRELAND.

IRISHMEN AND IRISHWOMEN: In the name of God and of the dead generations from which she receives her old tradition of nationhood, Ireland, through us, summons her children to her flag and strikes for her freedom.

Having organised and trained her manhood through her secret revolutionary organisation, the Irish Republican Brotherhood, and through her open military organisations, the Irish Volunteers and the Irish Citizen Army, having patiently perfected her discipline, having resolutely waited for the right moment to reveal itself, she now seizes that moment, and, supported by her exiled children in America and by gallant allies in Europe, but relying in the first on her own strength, she strikes in full confidence of victory.

We declare the right of the people of Ireland to the ownership of Ireland, and to the unfettered control of Irish destinies, to be sovereign and indefeasible. The long usurpation of that right by a foreign people and government has not extinguished the right, nor can it ever be extinguished except by the destruction of the Irish people. In every generation the Irish people have asserted their right to national freedom and sovereignty; six times during the past three hundred years they have asserted it in arms. Standing on that fundamental right and again asserting it in arms in the face of the world, we hereby proclaim the Irish Republic as a Sovereign Independent State, and we pledge our lives and the lives of our comrades-in-arms to the cause of its freedom, of its welfare, and of its exaltation among the nations.

The Irish Republic is entitled to and hereby claims, the allegiance of every Irishman and Irishwoman. The Republic guarantees religious and civil liberty, equal rights and equal opportunities to all its citizens, and declares its resolve to pursue the happiness and prosperity of the whole nation and of all its parts, cherishing all the children of the nation equally, and oblivious of the differences carefully fostered by an alien government, which have divided a minority from the majority in the past.

Until our arms have brought the opportune moment for the establishment of a permanent National Government, representative of the whole people of Ireland and elected by the suffrages of all her men and women, the Provisional Government, hereby constituted, will administer the civil and military affairs of the Republic in trust for the people.

We place the cause of the Irish Republic under the protection of the Most High God, Whose blessing we invoke upon our arms, and we pray that no one who serves that cause will dishonour it by cowardice, inhumanity, or rapine. In this supreme hour the Irish nation must, by its valour and discipline and by the readiness of its children to sacrifice themselves for the common good, prove itself worthy of the august destiny to which it is called.

Signed on Behalf of the Provisional Government,

THOMAS J. CLARKE.

SEAN Mac DIARMADA.   THOMAS MacDONAGH.
P. H. PEARSE.   EAMONN CEANNT,
JAMES CONNOLLY.   JOSEPH PLUNKETT.

Below: Sir Edward Carson (1854–1935) led the Northern Irish Resistance to the British Government's plans for Irish Home Rule. He is shown here speaking in Ireland. After the end of World War I he devoted his time to trying to find a compromise solution to the Irish problem.

Left: A Bolshevik demonstration on the streets of Petrograd (formerly St. Petersburg) in January 1917 during the days when the Kornilov uprising threatened the Provisional Government and Alexander Kerensky, its leader and deputy chairman of the Petrograd Soviet, was away on the Galician Front visiting the troops.

Below: Leon Trotsky, in the Astrakan cap, acknowledging the cheers of his supporters in Red Square, Moscow, on March 16, 1917. He had just returned to Russia after a period in exile when he worked as a revolutionary journalist in the West. Alongside Lenin, Trotsky played a major role in the Russian Revolution.

Above: Leon Trotsky (without the hat) on January 1, 1919, taking the salute from Red Army soldiers. He was a leading Bolshevik theorist and Commissar for War for the Red Army. From the October Revolution until the death of Lenin in 1924 Trotsky was the second most powerful man in the Soviet Union. But he had made a lot of enemies and was defeated by Stalin after a bitter power struggle. He was exiled to central Asia, but was then forced to leave altogether. He fled to Mexico in 1936 and was murdered at home there in 1940, probably by Soviet agents of Stalin.

Left: Keir Hardie (1856–1915), Scottish British Labour leader and politician, as he looked in November 1921. He was the first Parliamentary leader of the Labour Party.

Left: General Chiang Kai-shek (1887-1975), Chairman of the Kuomintang, President of the Republic of China (1928–31), head of the executive (1935–45), and Commander-in-Chief of the Nationalist Army opposing the Japanese. In 1948 he withdrew with his anti-Communist Kuomintang party to the island of Formosa (now Taiwan) where he formed the opposition Chinese national government. This photograph shows him in 1929.

Right: Jawaharlal Nehru, Indian statesman and nationalist leader. He spent several periods in prison—totalling 18 years—courtesy of the British for his nationalist activities. In 1928 he was elected president of the Indian National Congress. He followed a policy of non-cooperation with Britain during World War II although he was sympathetic to the Allied cause. He was the first Prime Minister of independent India (1947-1964) and Minister of External Affairs. He was the father of future Indian Prime Minister, Indira Gandhi.

POLITICAL CHANGE

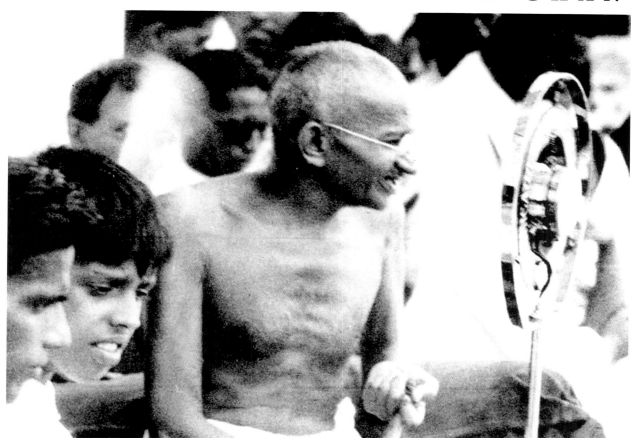

Left: Mahatma Gandhi (1869-1948), speaking into a microphone as he addresses a women's meeting in Bombay during a brief stay in the city in July 1931. Gandhi played a major part in the struggle for Home Rule for India and was frequently arrested for acts of civil disobedience against the British Raj. Gandhi became widely known as the man responsible for securing India's independence by leading a campaign of non-violent resistance to British rule for decades. But, on the day the sun finally set on the British Raj in India at the stroke of midnight on August 14, 1947, he could not rejoice for long. Jubilant scenes across the country quickly turned to horror— thousands died as bitter fighting erupted between Muslims and Hindus in the two new countries of India and Pakistan, created through the partition of the religiously divided sub-continent.

Right: Iosif Vissarionovich Dzhugashvili, better known as Josef Stalin, or Uncle Joe, (1879–1953). In 1932 when this photograph was taken Stalin had consolidated his position as Soviet leader following the death of Lenin in 1924, including the threat to his authority that Leon Trotsky posed. Many ordinary people opposed Stalin's reforms to the Soviet Union and many died as a consequence, especially in opposition to his agricultural policies. In 1932–33 up to ten million peasants died either because of execution or induced famines brought about by collectivization of agriculture. He also eliminated people accused of belonging to the right-wing intelligentsia and purged thousands in the officer corps who were believed to harbor German sympathies.

Left: In 1933 when this photograph was taken Adolf Hitler (1889–1945) had just become Chancellor of Germany. He had already spent nine months in Landesberg prison in 1923 for participation in trying to overthrow the Bavarian government. During that time he dictated his political testament *Mein Kampf* ("My Struggle") to Rudolf Hess. In the book—which was also his autobiography—he laid out many of his ideas for the future condition of Germany. Although unsuccessful in the presidential elections of 1932, Hitler joined the Cabinet the following year when he was made Chancellor—where the other politicians wrongly thought he could be controlled. Hitler was instrumental in plotting the burning of the Reichstag, the German seat of government in Berlin, and settling the blame on the Communists thereby causing a constitutional crisis which resulted in general elections. The Nazi Party scrapped a majority and Hitler took the reigns of power via the Enabling Acts. All opposition from within the Nazi Party was eliminated in the "Night of the Long Knives," June 1943, carried out by his SS bodyguard under the leadership of Reinhard Heydrich and Heinrich Himmler. This left Adolf Hitler as absolute and undisputed leader of Nazi Germany.

Right: The barbed wire fence surrounding the Auschwitz concentration camp near Krakow, Poland gives little indication of the horrors within. Even in 1945 at the end of the war most of the outside world had yet to learn of the sheer evil that these camps contained. The Nazi SS had established Auschwitz in 1940 and then expanded it into an extermination camp the following year. Soviet troops liberated the camp in January 1945 when this photograph was taken.

Above: The Prince of Wales (later Edward VIII, then after abdication, the Duke of Windsor) mounted on a Maharajah's champion pony on independence day for India. The sun set on scenes like this and on the end of the British Raj at the stroke of midnight on August 14, 1947.

Left: Mao Zedong, the Chairman of the Communist Party of China and leader of the People's Republic of China. In January 1949 when this picture was taken Mao had just become Chairman of the newly established People's Republic of China. He had gained power through the use of a massive peasant army who were in part motivated by the slogan "Political power grows through the barrel of a gun." Mao resigned the chairmanship in 1959 but remained chairman of the politburo and undisputed leader of China until his death in 1976 at the age of 83. As "father of the Chinese revolution" his *Little Red Book* was required reading for all Chinese citizens.

Above: Cuban counter-revolutionary members of Assault Brigade 2506, after their capture in the Bay of Pigs, Cuba, April 17, 1961. This incident was planned by the CIA and was one of the bitterest confrontations of the Cold War. This US. sponsored attempted invasion of Cuba by Cuban exiles led by José Cardona landed 1,500 men at Bahia de Cochinos (Bay of Pigs) on the southern coast of the island of Cuba. Their intention was the overthrow of the government of Fidel Castro and their expectation was that the population would rise to support them. Both objectives failed to occur. Cuban troops commanded by Fidel Castro rapidly overwhelmed and defeated the invaders. By April 20 all the men had been captured or killed.

Left: Arriving at Heathrow Airport, London, are Kenyan Asian children after flying in from Nairobi. In February 1968 the situation for non-Africans had got so dangerous in Kenya that thousands of Asians fled the country fearing for their lives. Most came to Britain as the former Commonwealth power where they were generally received with sympathy and help.

Left: The voting age in Britain was reduced from 21 to 18 and a new generation was entitled to vote for the first time in March 1970. Making electoral history is an 18 year old typist, Trudy Sellick of North Newton, Somerset, who is shown at the polling station in North Newton where she voted at 7am as the station opened. The Bridgwater election was the first since the voting age was reduced.

Right: Politician John Erlichman was a key figure in the Watergate scandal. In 1972 at the time of this photo he was President Richard Nixon's domestic affairs advisor until forced to resign from his post in 1973 following the Watergate scandal. In 1975 he was convicted for obstruction of justice, conspiracy, and perjury in connection with efforts to cover up the bungled burglary of the Democratic National committee offices at the Watergate complex in Washington.

Left: On May 4, 1979, Margaret Thatcher's Conservative Party won the general election and she became the first woman to hold the post of Prime Minister of Great Britain. She is seen waving to well-wishers at Tory Party headquarters after her stunning win. She told flag-waving supporters "My victory is greater than I had dared to hope."

Below: On November 10, 1989, the world watched in delighted astonishment as more than a million citizens of the German Democratic Republic streamed across the open border to West Germany. The Berlin Wall was pulled down within hours and Berliners were able to dance together in the streets for the first time in decades. East and West Germans were at long last reunited into one country.

POLITICAL CHANGE

Right: As news of the breach of the Berlin Wall spread like wildfire through the once divided city tens of thousands of Berliners went onto the streets to celebrate. A section of the wall was removed to ease the congestion of people wanting to cross the border following the announcement by East Germany two days earlier that "citizens are free to travel." The news sparked off days of celebrations with Berliners from East and West tearing down the wall that was erected overnight in August 1961.

Left: Protesters outside the South African Embassy in Trafalgar Square celebrating the announcement of the release of Nelson Mandela from jail in 1990. The protesters formed part of a non-stop vigil that had lasted outside the Embassy since April 19, 1986. Mandela was initially imprisoned in 1962 for five years for incitement, this was transmuted to life imprisonment under the Supression of Communism Act when he was found guilty of treason and sabotage in a further trial. He spent the first part of his imprisonment at the notorious high security prison on Robben Island. Mandela refused to cut a political deal with the South African authorities which would have given him his freedom. He was finally freed by the new South African president F. W. de Klerk following world wide requests for his release.

Left: South African National Congress (ANC) President Nelson Mandela and his then-wife Winnie Madikizela Mandela raise their fists on February 11, 1990, in Paarl to salute cheering crowds upon Mandela's release from Victor Verster prison. Nelson Mandela would soon turn 80 on July 18 amid a whirl of events to celebrate his path to freedom.

Below: The Conservative Thatcher government abolished council tax on houses and replaced it with a so-called poll tax. Instead of a standard charge this meant that each individual within a dwelling would be charged, therefore neighbours in identical houses could pay enormously different amounts depending on the number of people living in the house. This new tax was hugely unpopular and provoked riots and protests around the country. Here police officers in riot gear arrest a protester near the National Gallery, in Trafalgar Square, London, after a demonstration against the poll tax on March 31, 1990 developed into a riot. Mounted officers can be seen in the background, looking towards the Charing Cross Road.

Above: Released hostage Terry Waite sharing a joke with Lord Runcie (formerly Archbishop of Canterbury) at RAF Lynam on November 22, 1991. Waite was taken hostage in Beirut while working as the Archbishop's special envoy sent to discover the fate of various European hostages held in the Middle East and negotiate their release. He helped to free 14 hostages before he himself was taken hostage in January 1987. He was finally released on November 18, 1991.

Above: Fireworks light up Hong Kong's Victoria Harbour to mark the British withdrawal from the territory on June 30, 1997. At midnight Hong Kong was handed back to Chinese sovereignty at the expiry of the 99-year lease of the New Territories.

Far Right: A crowded street in San Sebastian, Spain where people gathered to protest against terrorism on Friday May 25, 2001, the day after Santiago Oleaga, chief financial officer of the newspaper *El Diario Vasco* was shot dead in San Sebastian, north Spain. His killing is widely blamed on the Basque separatist group ETA. The banner reads in Spanish and Basque "No ETA, Peace and Freedom."

Right: Holocaust survivors Tibor Vidal (center left, rear) and Margret Zentner (center right, rear) and US attorney Ed Fagan (right) visit the Paradeplatz in Zurich, April 23, 1998, while taking action against Swiss Banks and European Insurance Companies who hold their assets. The claimants are holding special "memorial services" in Zurich, Munich, Prague, Auschwitz/Birkenau, and Trieste in honor of the victims of the Nazis during World War II.

One of the greatest problems faced up to and tackled in the 20th century has been that of civil rights. In 1900 the world was still a very unequal place. The divide lay not just between rich and poor—still a major problem today—but between men and women, black and white, aristocrat and servant, homosexual and heterosexual rights.

Civil rights have a long history as people have struggled to be allowed a voice and equal status in their own country. Every nation has taken this at different speed—some willingly and some emphatically not. Many societies around the world are decidedly unequal, this tends to be true of very religious societies where human rights are suborned to the law of a higher design. But in the western, civilized world, most citizens, at least nominally, enjoy equal rights with their fellows no matter their sex, color, or creed.

The great civil rights issue of the early century predominantly concerned votes for women. Women had been agitating for equal rights with men for years but their demands mostly fell on deaf ears as men insisted on their prerogative of controlling all matters to do with politics as well as domestic life. On marriage a woman's property became that of her husband's and only in exceptional circumstances did she retain any control over it. The change came about following World War I when women took up jobs vacated by men sent to war and ran their homes and businesses without male support. When the men returned most were horrified to find their women unwilling to retreat back to the kitchen and were forced to concede that women deserved better legal recognition. A major political upheaval was underway.

Women first got the right to vote in Finland in 1916, while women in the US soon followed with the right to vote in 1920. Later still, in 1928 women in Britain got the right

CIVIL RIGHTS

to vote in Parliamentary elections, although married women had been allowed to vote in local elections since 1894. At last momentum for equal rights for women had gathered, but it took a long time for the majority of women in the world to be allowed to express their basic civil rights and vote in political elections.

The Civil Rights Movement, so called, was a political phenomenon of 1960s and 1970s America. The big issue was color segregation and the issue exploded in Montgomery, Alabama in December 1955 when Rosa Parks refused to give up her seat on on a bus to a white man. She was arrested and her local pastor, Martin Luther King Jr., rallied support for the cause. He was a truly charismatic leader who inspired thousands to follow him, his philosophy of non-violence and passive resistance helped to secure the Civil Rights Act of 1964 (for which he received the Nobel Peace Prize) and in 1965 the Voting Rights

Act. He was shamefully assassinated in Memphis, Tennessee in April 1968 but his death galvanized the movement and shamed those who worked against him.

In the later 1960s and early 1970s the civil rights movement also took on the cause of the anti-Vietnam war movement. This was of particular relevance to young men of draft age and their girl friends in colleges and university campuses across America who did not want to go to fight and die for a cause they didn't believe in, for a president (Nixon) they despised. When the war in the Far East was resolved the civil rights cause in the 1980s and 1990s changed to the contentious issue of gay rights. The anti-gay rights lobby predominantly came from right wing churchgoers who quoted scripture to help their cause. Their position became increasingly untenable and, generally speaking, gay rights are now securely upheld in most law-abiding countries around the world.

1955

Rosa Parks refuses to give up her seat on a bus to a white man. Leads to the Montgomery bus boycott and the activization of Dr Martin Luther King.

1957

Bitter dispute over integration in schools in Little Rock, Arkansas. 500 soldiers of 101st. Airborne Division sent by Eisenhower to preserve order.

Ineffectual Civil Rights Act passed by Congress.

1960

New Civil Rights Act somewhat increased power of Attorney-General to protect rights of African-American citizens to vote.

1960

Two African-American students start protest "Sit-in" movement in Greensboro, North Carolina.

1963

August 28. Martin Luther King "I have a dream . . ."

Betty Friedan publishes The Feminine Mystique — women need fulfillment thru good paid employment.

Civil rights march on Washington.

1964

July 2. President Johnson signs Civil Rights Act. Gave Attorney-General new powers to protect citizens rights. Outlawed segregation in public places, forbade federal racial discrimination.

Ku Klux Klan bombs 24 black churches and renews murdering campaign, including killing 1 black and 2 white young civil rights volunteers.

1965

Los Angeles race riots.

Malcolm X assassinated in Harlem by Black Muslim assassins.

1966

National Organization for Women (NOW) founded in Washington during Commissions on the Status of Women's conference.

Black Panther Party established.

Anti-Vietnam, mass draft protests in US.

1968

Martin Luther King Jr. assassinated.

Violence at Democratic National Convention, Chicago.

1969

Woodstock Festival for Music and Peace.

1970

May 1. Kent State University, Ohio, five protesting students shot and killed by National Guard.

1973

January 27. End of the US draft announced.

Abortion legalized in US.

1977

Steve Biko, founder and leader of South African Black Consciousness Movement and anti-apartheid campaigner, tortured to death in police custody.

1981

Sandra Day O'Connor becomes the first woman appointed to the US Supreme Court.

1984

"Coloreds" allowed to vote in South Africa.

1989

April 27. Protesting students massacred by Chinese Army in Beijing's Tiananmen Square. Unknown numbers of dead.

1991

South Africa Repeals Apartheid Laws

1992

Riots in Los Angeles after the Rodney King verdict clears police of murder.

Left: A Suffragette housemaid in 1908 during the campaign for the enfranchisement of women. The first women to get the vote were Finns in 1916, closely followed by American women in 1920. British women had been allowed to vote in local elections since 1894 but were only allowed to vote for members of Parliament from 1928.

Below: Leading Suffragette campaigner Emily Pankhurst addressing a meeting in London's Trafalgar Square, October 11, 1908.

Left: Leading British Suffrage campaigner, Sylvia Pankhurst, at her desk in 1911. The following year she moved to the poverty-stricken docklands area of east London where she set up the East London Federation of the Suffragettes.

Below: Suffragettes became so politically active and inventive in their protests that even the royal family needed protection from their actions. For a garden party at Buckingham Palace in July 1919, a squad of women police officers were positioned at the Duke of York steps in anticipation of trouble.

Above: The Lancashire contingent of the Hunger Marchers passing through Gerrards Cross, Buckinghamshire, on October 25, 1932.

Right: Jeanette Rankin (1880-1973), the first woman member of the House of Representatives, and an active suffragette and social worker, in a photograph taken in 1940. She was a Republican from Montana and an active pacifist and voted against US entry into World War I and then against joining the Allies in World War II even after the events at Pearl Harbor. She lost her seat in 1942.

Right: In 1948 President Harry Truman proclaimed February 1st. the anniversary of the passage of the 13th Amendment to the Constitution—which outlawed slavery—as "National Freedom Day." Looking on are from left to right: Mrs. Harriet Lemons, J.E. Mitchell, Mary McCleod Bethune, E.C. Wright, Dr. C. Jernagin, and Elder Michaux.

Below: The "March on Washington for Jobs and Freedom" on August 28, 1963 was supported by many Americans wanting better civil rights. Over 200,000 people of all ethnicities marched through Washington to protest. The leaders met President John F Kennedy, to explain their grievances, including Roy Wilkins (left) and Walter White of the National Association for the Advancement of Colored People (NAACP). On the right is Thurgood Marshall, leading counsel for the NAACP, who was heavily involved in civil rights legal actions—especially segregation in schools—and later became the first African-American Justice of the Supreme Court.

Right: The first African-Americans to tee off at one of Atlanta's previously all-white public golf courses. C.T. Bell, Alfred "Tup" Holmes, and his brother Oliver W. Holmes, walk away from the green after playing nine holes at North Fulton Golf course. The Holmes brothers had instituted the legal action that led to the Supreme Court ruling ordering public golf courses open to all citizens, and thus reversing two lower court decisions. The golf pro at the course reported no reaction among white players and "no incidents" on this historic day, December 28, 1955.

Left: Daisy Bates and President Clarence Laws, reading the official letter from the Supreme Court giving its unanimous decision to proceed with integration at Central High School, September 12, 1958.

CIVIL RIGHTS

Left: Civil Rights marches took place all over America in the early 1960s.

Below: Medgar Evers, state NAACP field secretary, speaks about race relations during a television broadcast on May 20, 1963. Evers was the civil rights leader in Mississippi and he was murdered later that year by his enemies.

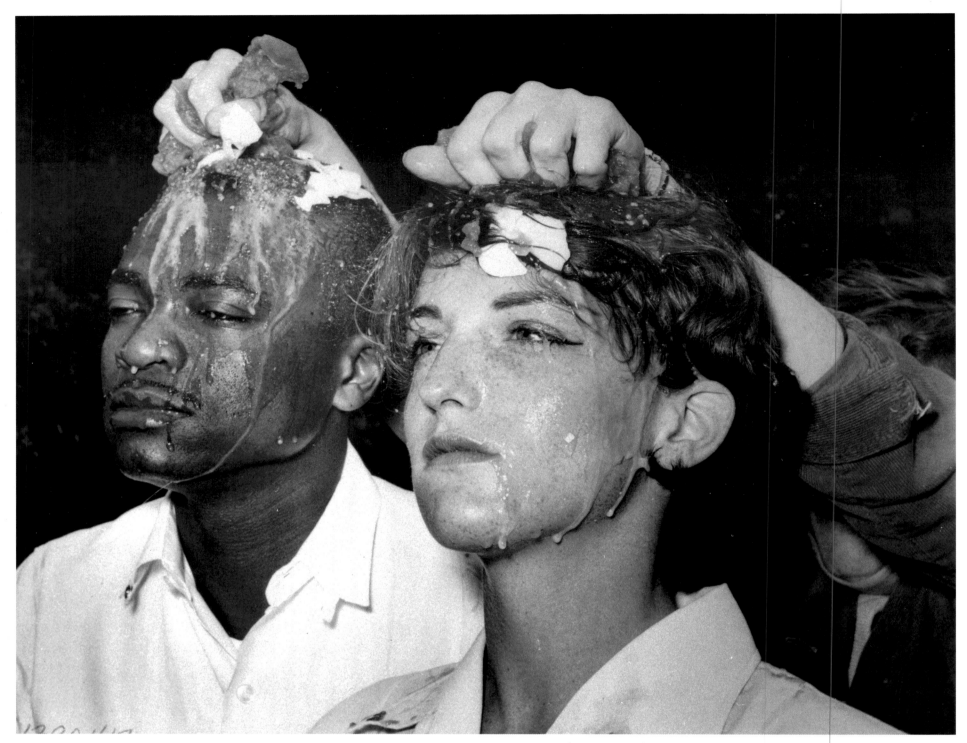

Above: Civil rights protesters had to be prepared to meet hostility in response to their actions. Consequently, some chapters conducted workshops in nonviolent demonstration tactics and seminars on picketing techniques and responding passively to aggression. Here a couple of trainees, Richard Siller and Lois Bonzell of the Congress of Racial Equality (CORE) maintain their stoic posture as they submit to an egg shampoo for civil rights

Right: Anti-apartheid protesters marching through London from Hyde Park to the rallying point in Trafalgar Square, November 3, 1963.

Right: Supported by her husband, Mrs. Robert Goodman is overcome with grief as the body of her son arrives at Newark Airport in New Jersey on August 7, 1964. The Goodman's son was one of three civil rights workers slain in Mississippi by members of the Ku Klux Klan.

Left: Julian Bond speaking at a press conference at the Hotel Drake in New York City in January 1966. A year earlier he was denied his seat in the Georgia State Legislature although he had been legally elected because of his objection to the United States' participation in the Vietnam War. Voters in his district re-elected him twice, but he was still denied his seat until the Supreme Court ruled his exclusion unconstitutional in December, 1966. Bond was sworn into office on January 9, 1967 and served in the Georgia House of Representatives until 1975 and in the Georgia Senate from 1975 until 1987.

Left: 1968 demonstration against the Vietnam War in Grosvenor Square, London. This is one of the largest squares in London which was very useful for rallies at this time as Grosvenor Square is also the site of the American Embassy and so the focus for anti-Vietnam protests.

Below: Harlem Congressman Adam Clayton Powell Jr. and Congresswoman Shirley Chisolm of Brooklyn give the clenched fist Black Power salute during a parade in Harlem on September 21, 1969. This was the first Afro-American parade in New York, a city celebrated for ethnic demonstrations.

Above: Roger Baldwin, the founder back in January 1920 of the American Civil Liberties Union (ACLU). The union was formed as "a permanent, national, nonpartisan organization with the single purpose of defending the whole Bill of Rights for everybody." Baldwin, seen here in January 1970, was visiting the US Supreme Court in Washington. The following day he was in New York for the anniversary of the foundation of the ACLU on January 21st. 300 civil libertarians honored Baldwin at the Americana Hotel in a dual party, celebrating his 86th birthday and the 50th anniversary of the ACLU.

Right: Aspiring magician Diane Matthews protesting against sex discrimination by burning her bra outside the Magic Circle in Chenies Mews, London. She had been refused entry in 1972 after being told that only men are eligible to join the circle. Bra burning, however, was more a metaphor for women's freedom than a reality.

Left: Russell Means of the American Indian Movement (AIM), was the spokesman for rebel Native Americans at Wounded Knee, South Dakota, on March 5, 1973.

Below: American Indian Movement (AIM) leaders Russell Means (seated at left) and Dennis Banks (seated wearing vest) sing an AIM victory song with other members at a victory rally on September 17, 1974. The rally was held after charges were dismissed against Banks and Means in the eight-month-long Wounded Knee trial.

Left: One of the last civil rights issues to be tackled was gay rights. Here the Reverend Malcolm Boy and his lover John Due cuddle on a some beanbags in February 1978 in open celebration of their sexuality.

Right: Expressing his support for the legalise cannabis campaign, a demonstrator relaxes with a joint in London's Hyde Park while taking part in a protest rally organized by the Smoky Bears—the direct action wing of the group. May 12, 1979.

Above: RAF Greenham Common air base was the site of continuous women's peace protests from 1981 until 1991 when the final American Cruise missiles were removed. The demonstrations ended when the base was finally closed. The fence surrounding Greenham Common for over 50 years was pulled down, marking a final victory for peace campaigners.

Left: Massive police presence greets pickets as they arrive on the hill heading to the Orgreave Coking Plant near Rotherham, Yorkshire, during the bitter miners dispute of 1984.

Above: Australian feminist writer Germaine Greer was in Helsinki to promote her latest book *The Change* in March 1993. Her seminal work, *The Female Eunuch* was published in 1970 making her an internationally known figure renowned for being at the forefront of feminist issues.

Right: Convicted prisoners have their civil rights—such as the right to vote—suspended for the duration of their sentence, as 87 year old Maurice Papon discovered for himself. Found guilty by a French court in 1998 he was sentenced to ten years for crimes against humanity for his role in the deportation of Jews during World War II.

1901

February 27. Russian Minister of Education Bogolepov, to avenge repression of student activists.

September 14. William McKinley, 25th President of the US, by Léon F Czolgosz, an anarchist, in Buffalo, New York.

1908

February 1. King Carlos I of Portugal and the Crown Prince, in Lisbon.

1910

February 20. Butros Ghali, Egyptian premier, by a Nationalist fanatic.

1913

March 18. King George I of Greece, at Salonika.

1914

June 28. Archduke Franz Ferdinand of Austria. Shot in Sarajevo by Serbian nationalist Gavrilo Princip. Ensuing turmoil started World War I.

1916

October 21. Austrian premier, Count Carl Stürgkh.

1919

February 21. Kurt Eisner, Bavarian premier, in Munich.

1920

May 20. President Venustiano Carranza of Mexico, killed by soldiers while fleeing on horseback.

1921

November 4. Prime Minister of Japan, Hara Kei, by ultra-nationalist fanatic.

1930

November 14. Prime Minister Hamaguchi of Japan, shot by right-wing fanatic. Died following year.

1932

May 6. President Paul Doumer of France, by a Russian émigré.

1933

December 29. Ion Duca, premier of Romania, by the Iron Guard.

1934

July 25. Engelbert Dollfuss Austrian political leader, in a Nazi putsch in Vienna.

October 9. King Alexander of Yugoslavia, in Marseilles by Croatian terrorists alongside . . .

October 9. Jean Louis Barthou, French Foreign Minister.

December 1. Sergei Kirov, revolutionary and Stalin collaborator, in Leningrad. Led to widespread purges in the Russian Communist Party.

1939

September 21. Armand Calinescu, premier of Romania, by the Iron Guard.

1940

Leon Trotsky, Russian revolutionary, with an ice pick by Ramon del Rio while in exile in Mexico City.

1942

May 31. Deputy Protector of Bohemia and Moravia, Gestapo leader Reinhard Heydrich, by Czech patriots. The village of Lidice was razed and all the men murdered in reprisal.

December 24. French Admiral F. Darlan in Algiers. Leaving the way clear for De Gaulle to become leader of the Free French.

1945

February 24. Ahmed Pasha, premier of Egypt, after announcing declaration of war against Germany.

1948

January 30. Mahatma Ghandi, pacifist leader of India and hero of independence, in Delhi by Hindu fanatic.

September 17. Count Folke Bernadotte, the U.N. mediator in Palestine, by Jewish terrorists.

The dictionary definition of assassination is "to murder premeditatedly and treacherously" (Random House Dictionary). Assassination is the unlawful killing of a prominent—usually taken to mean political—person. One of the most defining moments of the 20th century was the assassination of Archduke Franz Ferdinand of Austria on June 28, 1914. Thanks to the Byzantine complexity of Balkan politics this was the crucial action that plunged Europe, and ultimately much of the world, into World War I.

In the first year of the new century the 25th President of the US, William McKinley was assassinated by Leon F. Czolgosz, an anarchist, while in Buffalo, New York. Then 62 years later on November 22, 1963, the 35th President of the US, John F. Kennedy was shot while in Dallas, Texas, allegedly by Lee Harvey Oswald. America and the world

mourned. Unlike previous high profile assassinations this was seen live on television and then again and again in endless repeats.

America was again plunged into horror when on April 4, 1968. the civil rights campaigner Martin Luther King Jr. was assassinated in Memphis, Tennessee, by James Earl Ray. His death galvanized the civil rights movement and the demand for an end to segregation in America. Barely had this atrocity left the front pages of the newspapers when Robert Kennedy, the brother of the dead president and Democratic nominee for the White House, was assassinated after winning the California primary on June 5, 1968. His assassin was a Palestinian immigrant, Sirhan Sirhan.

In spite of all the talk of conspiracy theories, nothing has come to light to prove that either the assassinations of John and Robert Kennedy or the attempts on George Wallace, Ronald Reagan, and Gerald Ford, are anything other than the work of lone madmen.

ASSASSINATIONS

Elsewhere the assassins' bombs and bullets have worked to great effect to provoke turmoil and insurgency. On January 30, 1948, the great Indian leader, Mahatma Gandhi, was assassinated in Delhi by a Hindu fanatic. Although he advocated peace and passive resistance his death led to even greater mistrust and bloodshed between Hindus and Muslims. Although India is the largest democracy in the world, politics is never calm. Matters were brought to boiling point over 40 years later by the assassination of the prime minister Indira Gandhi on October 31, 1984, by members of her Sikh bodyguard. One of the consequences was the subsequent murder of around 3,000 Sikhs in Delhi.

Maybe peace in the Middle East was the price paid when on October 31, 1984, the president of the United Arab Republic of Egypt, Anwar el-Sadat, was assassinated by

Muslim extremists while reviewing troops. Sadat had been deeply involved in the peace process between the Arabs and Israelis and had been awarded a joint Nobel Peace Prize with the Israeli prime minister Menachem Begin. With his death Middle East politics became more fractured than ever and despite many people's best intentions, peace has never settled on the area.

More recently the assassination of the Dutch nationalist leader and candidate in the elections, Pim Fortuyn, in May 2002 by an animal rights activist altered the Dutch political landscape—at least for a time. The assassination provoked outrage and general sympathy among the Dutch public, Pim became an instant political martyr and his party the List Pim Fortuyn party was voted into a power sharing three-party coalition. His death provoked considerable sympathy and put a political party into a position of power that had no real hope of otherwise gaining control.

1951
March 7. Razmara, premier of Iran.

July 20. King Abdullah of Jordan, in Jordan.

October 6. British High Commissioner in Malaya, Henry Gurney.

October 16. Ali Khan, Prime Minister of Pakistan.

1958
July 14. King Feisal of Iraq, during coup d'état in Baghdad.

1959
September 25. S. Bandaranaike, Prime Minister of Ceylon (Sri Lanka), by a Buddhist monk.

1960
August 29. Premier of Jordan, Hazza el-Majali.

1963
November 1. President Ngo Dinh Diem, in army coup, in Vietnam.

November 22. John F Kennedy, President of the US by Lee Harvey Oswald, in Dallas.

November 24. Lee Harvey Oswald, JFK's assassin, shot by Jack Ruby.

1965
February 21. Black leader Malcom X, by Black Muslim assassins, in Harlem, New York.

1966
September 6. Dr Hendrik Verwoerd, South African Prime Minister, in the House of Assembly, Cape Town.

1968
April 4. Martin Luther King, civil rights leader and Baptist clergyman, in Memphis, by James Earl Ray.

June 5 (shot) died June 6. Robert Kennedy, former Attorney-General and Democratic presidential candidate, by Jordanian immigrant, Sirhan Sirhan.

1969
Tom Mboya, Kenyan trade unionist and politician.

1979
November 26. President Park Chung-Hee of Korea, by the head of the Korean central intelligence service.

1981
October 6. President Anwar Sadat of the United Arab Republic of Egypt, by Muslim extremists while reviewing his troops.

1983
Benigno Aquino, Filipino opposition politician, on his return to the Philippines, by a military guard at Manila airport.

1984
October 31. Indira Gandhi, Indian Prime Minister, by members of her Sikh bodyguard.

1986
February 28. Olof Palme, Prime Minister of Sweden. Shot in the center of Stockholm while walking home from the cinema with his wife.

1991
May 21. Rajiv Gandhi, former Indian Prime Minister, while campaigning, by a bomb hidden a woman's dress as she handed him flowers.

1995
November 4. Itzhak Rabin, Israeli Prime Minister, by Israeli extremist while at a peace rally in Tel Aviv.

2001
January 16. Congo president Laurent Kabila, by his bodyguard.

2002
May. Dutch nationalist politician Pim Fortuyn, by animal rights activist.

2003
March 27. Zoran Djindjic, Serbian Prime Minister, by Mile "Kum" Lukovic and Dusan Spasojevic-Siptar, alleged leaders of a mafia-linked group who were shot by Belgrade police in a shootout.

Left: The last photograph taken of President William McKinley at Buffalo, New York, September 6, 1901. Three hours after this picture was taken, Léon Czolgosz, a fanatic anarchist, fired the shots while waiting in the handshaking reception line at the Buffalo Exhibition. At the right is John G. Wilburn, the President's host in Buffalo, and at whose house he died eight days later on September 14. At the left is James L. Wilson, who was Secretary of Agriculture in Mr. McKinley's cabinet.

Below: Archduke Franz Ferdinand of Austria was assassinated (as was his wife, Sophie) on Sunday June 28, 1914, in Sarajevo by Gavrilo Princip, a Serbian nationalist revolutionary. This atrocity led directly to the outbreak of World War I thanks to the complicated network of alliances and agreements between the countries of Europe.

Above: Earlier in 1914, Archduke Franz Ferdinand of Austria posed with his wife, Duchess Sophie, and their children (left to right) Maximilian (the eldest), Ernst, and Sophie.

Left: Gavrilo Princip, the 19-year-old student led a group of young Serbian nationalists known as the "Black Hand." Their aim was independence for the southern Slav peoples from the governing Austro-Hungarian Empire. The group shot down the Archduke Franz Ferdinand and his wife, Sophie and within six weeks Europe was in turmoil. Princip was pursued and caught and sentenced to 20 years in prison. However, he only served four years before dying in 1918 of tuberculosis in an Austrian prison.

Left: The "Mad Monk" Grigori Efimovich Rasputin was the focus of much hatred and resentment for his influence over the Imperial family of Russia and over the Empress Alexandra in particular. She was fascinated with him in his guise as a Siberian mystic whose skill appeared to help Alexis, the hemophiliac heir to the throne. Rasputin's influence stretched to political and clerical appointments which aroused the consequent jealousy and resentment of the court. His drinking and general licentious behavior disgusted the nobles (boyars) in particular and a clique of loyal aristocratic monarchists led by Prince Felix Yusupov finally managed to kill him on December 29, 1916. This was not so easy, first they poisoned him, and when that failed they shot him, but he still survived so they tossed him into the freezing River Neva to be sure.

Below: The body of revolutionary general Pancho Villa, laid out at the Fidalgo Hotel in Parral, Mexico after his assassination. Villa was shot at his nearby ranch on June 20, 1923.

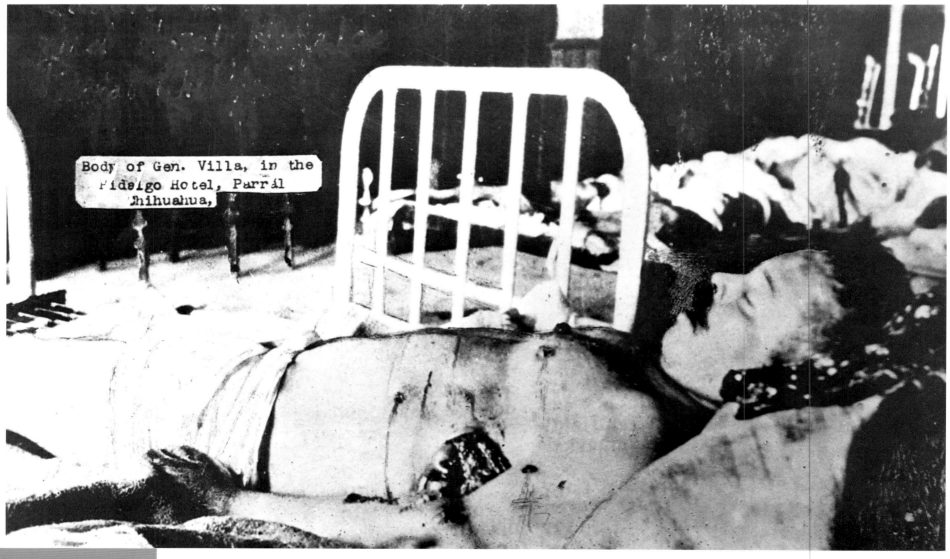

Body of Gen. Villa, in the Fidalgo Hotel, Parral Chihuahua,

ASSASSINATIONS

Above: One of the last public appearances of Inuaki Tsuyoki, Japanese prime minister on May 23, 1932. Wearing top hat and frock coat he is seen with members of the Cabinet attending Japan's Army Day Celebration in Tokyo. He had become prime minister in December 1931 at the time of the Manchurian crisis and had tried to curb the excesses of the notorious Japanese armed forces, so making himself very unpopular in those circles. Six months later—a few days after this picture was taken—he was assassinated on May 16, by a group of military officers. He was 77 years old and his successor, admiral Viscount Makoto Saito was 73 years old.

Left: Just a few minutes after President Sanchez Cerro of Peru had been assassinated by Abelardo Hurtado de Mendoza on May 8, 1933 in Lima, Peru. The assassin was soon shot dead by the angry crowd and troops had to bundle Mendoza's accomplices into a car and drive them to the safety of prison in Lima.

Above: Police chase after the assassins of King Alexander I of Yugoslavia killed during a state visit to Marseille. Alexander had become king of the Serbs, Croats and Slovenes in 1921 and was determined to build a strong and unified country. He and the French Foreign Minister, Jean Louis Barthou were killed in Marseilles on January 1, 1934. Barthou had invited Alexander to France on a state visit with the intention of strengthening French links with Eastern Europe against the growing expansionist threat of Germany. They were assassinated by Macedonian terrorists in the pay of Croatian nationalists.

ASSASSINATIONS

Above: On July 16, 1936 there was an attempted assassination on a member of the Royal Family. King Edward VIII escaped unharmed when a man in the crowd near Wellington Arch, London, produced a revolver. The man was immediately arrested by police and identified as George Andrew McMahon. Confidential documents disclosed in 2003 for the first time by the Public Record Office detail how George Andrew McMahon had intended to shoot himself in front of the king as he made his way back to Buckingham Palace via Constitution Hill after reviewing the Guards.

Left: Mohandas Karamchand Gandhi, better known as Mahatma Gandhi, photographed not long before his untimely death. He was assassinated by a Muslim fanatic in Delhi on January 30, 1948. He was a great and lasting influence for peace but unfortunately his desire to see Indians living caste free with complete religious tolerance has failed to materialize as the Indian sub-continent remains in constant religious turmoil as it has done for centuries.

Left: A priest stands by as a Chilean firing squad takes aim at Jorge del Carmen Valenzuela Torres, "The Jackal of Nahueltoro." His nickname was acquired when his dreadful crimes were discovered, on August 20, 1960. Aged 23, illiterate and miserable, he had killed his older live-in lover and her five daughters, using sticks and stones and even his feet to kill the youngest, who was only a few months old. After trial he was condemned to death by firing squad. The position of his heart is marked on his clothes with a red circle. Traditionally, one member of the firing squad has a blank cartridge in his rifle.

Below: Reporters inspect the bullet-ridden car in which Dominican dictator Rafael Trujillo was assasinated in June 1961. The automobile contained about 60 bullet holes and had blood stains on the back seat where Trujillo was seated. The Dominican authorities reported that two of the assassins had been killed in a gun battle with security police. One of the dead men was Juan Tomas Diaz, who was identified as the leader of the plot.

Above: Just before 12.30pm, November 22, 1963. President John F. Kennedy, First Lady Jacqueline Kennedy, and Texas Governor John Connally ride in a motorcade through Dallas, Texas. Moments later the president and governor were shot by an assassin, later alleged to be Lee Harvey Oswald, a dishonorably discharged former US marine. He was found to be a Marxist with a fascination for the Soviet Union. Oswald had traveled there in 1960 and applied for citizenship, instead, he was given permission to remain as a resident alien. Living in Minsk he worked in a local factory and married a Soviet girl, Marina Prusakova, in 1961. They soon moved to the US where they settled in Fort Worth, Texas. Oswald was himself shot by Jack Ruby, a shady Dallas night club owner two days after JFK's assassination and before any clear answers about his motivation or possible accomplices could be established. Ruby died in prison in 1967 while awaiting a retrial for murder.

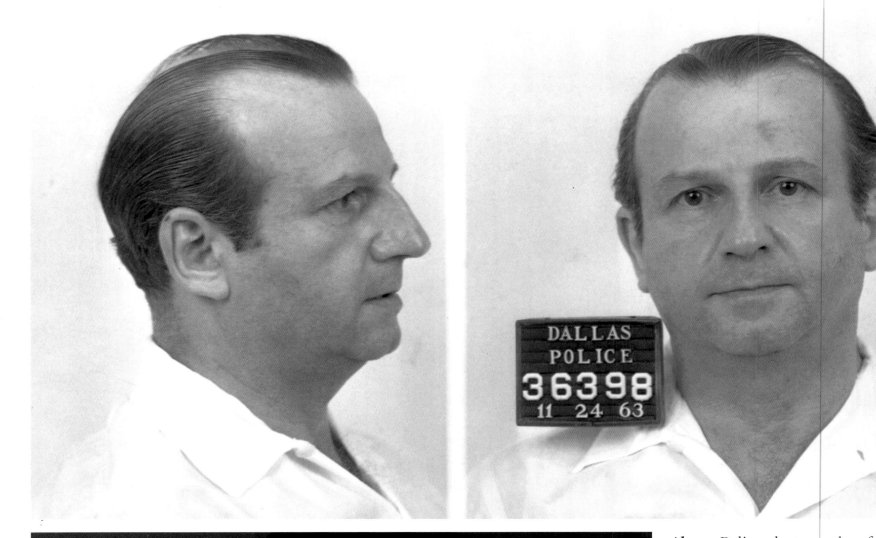

Above: Police photographs of Jack Ruby, arrested for murdering Lee Harvey Oswald as he was being moved from Dallas police station. The incident was caught live on television on November 24, 1963. Ruby strongly denied that he was involved in any conspiracy—however, every single aspect of the Kennedy assassination is layered in conspiracy theories.

Left: On February 21, 1965, Malcolm X former leader of the Black Muslim Sect was shot dead while addressing an OAAU (Afro-American Unity) rally in Harlem, New York. He was 39 and had just returned from a trip to London. He had been barred from entering France because it was believed his presence might cause demonstrations and create trouble as his philosophy was to use arms and violence to fight social injustice. His three assassins, at least two of whom were Black Muslims, regarded Malcolm X as a traitor to the cause.

ASSASSINATIONS

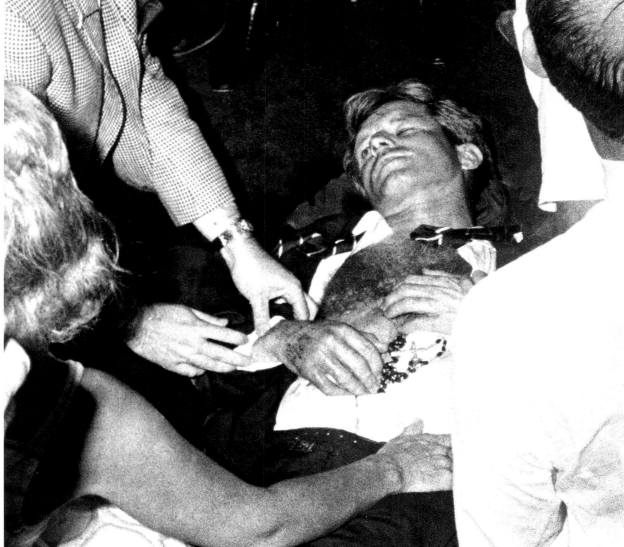

Above: Civil rights leader and Baptist minister Martin Luther King Jr. waving to his enthusiastic supporters on August 28, 1963, on the Mall in Washington D.C., during the 200,000 strong "March on Washington." Martin Luther King was the leader of the moral fight against racism in America but his nonviolent views were denigrated by more militant black activists. He was supporting a group of striking sanitation workers in Memphis when he was fatally shot at his motel by James Earl Ray, a hired assassin on April 4, 1968. Ray was convicted of Martin Luther King Jr.'s murder in 1969 and jailed for 99 years.

Left: Clutching his rosary beads, Senator Robert F. Kennedy lies wounded and dying on the floor of the Ambassador Hotel. He had just won the California primary election and was leaving the victory rally through the kitchens when he was shot by Sirhan Sirhan. His wife Ethel is seen at lower left.

Right: Assassinated presidential candidate Robert Kennedy. Former Attorney-General for his brother JFK, Robert Kennedy was especially active in pursuing civil rights and eliminating corruption from American business life, in the process he made many powerful enemies. At his brother's death Robert resigned his post and was elected Senator for New York in 1965. A lot of pressure was put on him to put himself up for the Democratic nomination and in 1968 Robert reluctantly agreed to run for president, ticketed as an idealist reformer. He was on course for possible victory when he was assassinated.

Left: Member of the British royal family, Lord Louis Mountbatten of Burma was killed by an IRA bomb on August 27, 1979 while sailing in Donegal Bay near his holiday home in County Sligo, Ireland. Mountbatten had had a distinguished military and diplomatic career and had served as (among many other duties) chief of UK Defence Staff (1959–65) and from 1953 had been personal aide-de-camp to Queen Elizabeth II.

Above: The reviewing stand at a military parade where Anwar Sadat was sitting when Muslim extremist assassins in the parade fired machine guns and threw grenades at him. October 6, 1981.

Right: Mile "Kum" Lukovic (left) and Dusan Spasojevic-Siptar, the two alleged leaders of a mafia-linked group suspected of assassinating Serbian prime minister Zoran Djindjic. The same day they were both killed in a shootout with police in Belgrade as they tried to resist arrest on March 27, 2003.

Terrorism is not a new phenomenon, but 20th century terrorism certainly made use of the latest technology to advance its disparate causes. For most people in the Western world there is something abhorrent in the sheer profligacy of terrorism: in a world where the military strives for greater and greater accuracy, worries about "collateral damage," and agonizes about casualties, the suicidal terrorist seems even more unfathomable. Choosing soft targets for maximum impact, the terrorist is the bogeyman for today, striking, it seems, randomly and without justification.

Of course, there is another point of view. Every terrorist is a freedom fighter; every murderer of innocent civilians is using force because the normal democratic means have failed. Were the assassins of Richard Heydrich, the beast of Moravia and proponent of

the Final Solution, terrorists? And when did the Israelis move from being the terrorists who perpetuated such outrages as the bombing of the King David Hotel to innocent victims of Palestinian terrorists? These are complex issues that are rarely worked out through diplomacy or politics. From the letter bomb to hijacking and assassination, direct action has the advantage of cutting through the verbiage of politicians—but does the threat of force ever solve a problem? The 20th century has had its quota of successful revolutions and rebellions—the British Empire jailed as terrorists many of those who would go on to run the countries in which they had performed their terrorist acts. But would those countries, and all the others that fought for independence, have achieved what they wanted without violence? History will tell whether such groups as the

TERRORISM

Basques, the Corsicans, the Chechens, or the Palestinians will eventually achieve what they are fighting for, and whether the ends justify the means. It can be difficult without the perspective of history to differentiate between the sponsors of state terrorism—the so-called axis of evil—and their opponents. The infants in the hospitals of Baghdad who were wounded by Allied bombs look very similar to those in the hospitals in Jerusalem put there by Palestinian terrorists.

The century started with terrorism in the Balkans; indeed, Europe was drawn into a massive conflagration as a result of it. It ended the century with these issues unresolved—and exacerbated by tit for tat revenge reprisals. Elsewhere, the retreat of empires was hastened by terrorism but as the terrorists took power, they ruled with a

similar disregard for law, democracy, and justice. Mugabe's Zimbabwe, Pol Pot's Cambodia, Saddam's Iraq—all of these statesmen turned tyrant when given power, often by the nations who had supported them. The background of arms' sales and financial support to Saddam Hussein, Osama Bin Laden, and so many others makes very embarrassing reading to those whose support was expedient at the time.

However, in the end the most lasting image of terrorism is the sheer waste: the callous disregard for human life; the completely amoral and antisocial world view that makes a cause more important than a child; the indoctrination of young men and women to kill themselves and others around them.

Hizballah suicide bombers attack barracks in Beirut 299 killed, including 241 US Marines.
Shi'ite suicide bombing of US embassy in Kuwait.

1984
IRA bomb the Grand Hotel, Brighton, nearly killing British Prime Minister Thatcher and her cabinet.
Truck bomb exploded outside the Aukar, Lebanon annex of the US embassy. 24 people killed.
Bin Laden founds Maktab al-Khidamat (MAK) to organize anti-Soviet rebels. The CIA donates $3 billion funds to the MAK.

1985
Italian cruise ship *Achille Lauro* hijacked.
Terrorists bomb the airports in Vienna and Rome killing 20.

1986
West Berlin disco bombed. In retaliation President Reagan orders bombing of Benghazi and Tripoli.

1987
Hostage negotiator Terry Waite taken hostage in Beirut, Lebanon. He will be released in November 1991.
Founding of Hamas, an acronym for the Islamic Resistance Movement.
IRA bomb at Enniskillen.

1988
Bin Laden starts al Qaeda (the Base).
A bomb onboard Pan Am 747 explodes over Lockerbie, Scotland, killing 270 (259 aboard and 11 town residents).
British SAS kills three IRA terrorists on active duty in Gibraltar.

1991
Car bomb explodes in basement of World Trade Center.

1992
Osama bin Laden proposes to Hizballah that they cooperate to killing United States troops stationed in Asia and Africa.
Bin Laden establishes legal businesses in Sudan as fronts for al Qaeda camps.
Hizballah agents bomb Israeli embassy in Argentina.

1994
Saudi Arabia revoke bin Laden's citizenship.
Hizballah agents bomb an Israeli cultural center in Buenos Aires, Argentina.

1995
The Islamic Jihad bombs the Egyptian embassy in Pakistan
Japanese Aum cult terrorists release Sarin nerve gas into Tokyo subway trains. 12 killed and 5,000 injured.
Timothy McVeigh causes truck bombing of Federal Building in Oklahoma City, killing 168.
Truck bombing of US National Guard training center in Riyadh, Saudi Arabia kills seven.

1996
Bomb in Dhahran, Saudi Arabia, kills 19 US military.

1997
Bin Laden says in CNN interview, "We declared a jihad against the United States because it is unjust, criminal, and tyrannical."

1998
US Embassies Nairobi and Dar es Salaam bombed: 224 people killed and almost 5,000 injured. US bombards locations in Afghanistan in retaliation.
On two separate days, Chechen terrorists bombed apartment buildings in Moscow, Russia. 212 were killed.

2000
Start of the New Intifada, a Palestinian rebellion against Israeli occupation
Suicide bombing of the USS Cole. 17 US sailors killed.

2001
ETA blast central Madrid In its 33-year terror campaign, ETA has killed around 800 people.
Bombing of a disco in Tel Aviv, Israel killed 21 people.
9-11 World Trade Center towers destroyed by hijacked aircraft. Another hits Pentagon. Missing persons list currently 4,979 missing, 393 confirmed dead.
Dissident Republicans' bomb in West Ealing, London.

2002
Bali bombings kill nearly 200.
Chechen rebels take 763 hostages in Moscow theater; Russian authorities release a gas into theater, killing 116 hostages and freeing remainder.

2003
Three terrorist bombs in Saudi Arabia kill 34 people.
Suicide bombers at the Farah Hotel and other locations in Casablanca kill 40.

Above: Members of the German ultra-left terrorist group, the Red Army Faction (RAF)—from left to right: Thorwald Proll, Horst Soehnlein, Andreas Baader, and Gudrun Ensslin—waiting for judgment at the Frankfurt am Main district court. The four were accused of arson on two Frankfurt department stores. The RAF announced its dissolution in a letter to a press agency confirmed by the federal prosecutor's office. But the prosecutor's office said the letter had yet to be verified by criminal police. The eight-page letter said, "Today we end this project. The urban guerilla battle of the RAF is now history."

Right: Astrid Proll, 32, former member of the Baader-Meinhof terrorist organization, after her release from custody in Frankfurt at the start of her trial for attempting to kill two officials in 1971, taking part in a bank raid in West Berlin, and using forged documents.

TERRORISM

Above: A dark mushroom cloud of smoke drifts across the centre of Belfast, as firemen hose down the remains of Oxford Street bus station, on July 21, 1972—Bloody Friday, when 27 bombs were detonated in Northern Ireland. Approaching the anniversary, 30 years later, the IRA apologized, for the killing of all "noncombatants" who died during its campaign of terror. The IRA added that it acknowledged the grief and pain of the families of the combatants—police, soldiers, and loyalist paramilitaries—killed during the violence. Records show the IRA killed nearly 1,800 people during its terror campaign, close on 650 of them civilians.

Right: Men of 1st Battalion Welsh Guards carry a bag of gelignite they found in a bomb factory they uncovered in a terraced house in Belfast's Keegan Street during a dawn swoop, July 26, 1972.

Above: The classic view of terrorism—hooded and masked. These photographs show two of the terrorists who penetrated into the Israeli accommodation in Munich's Olympic village in 1972. First, they held the sportsmen hostage, demanding the release of other terrorists from jail. Then they demanded a getaway helicopter. At the airport German antiterrorist operations went wrong and the ensuing melee saw eleven Israeli sportsmen, five terrorists, and a policeman die.

Right: The wreckage left at the "Tavern in the Town" in Birmingham after a bomb exploded in an underground bar, November 21, 1974. Because the blast was confined inside a basement, casualties and damage were particularly serious. "Soft" targets such as crowded bars are an easy target for terrorists: they lead to large amounts of publicity for their cause, maximum impact, with little chance of capture unless the state imposes draconian measures of stop and search. If it does so, the inconvenience caused is seen as another good result for the terrorist. The publicity makes fund raising—for the IRA mainly in areas of historic Irish immigration such as the United States—much easier.

TERRORISM

Left: Death and destruction in Birmingham, England, on August 21, 1974, when 21 died and 159 others were injured in the terror bombings of two city center pubs, the "Mulberry Bush" and the "Tavern in the Town." Six men are convicted in 1975, but the so-called Birmingham Six were released after 16 years in jail when their convictions were overturned by the Court of Appeal in May 1991.

Below: On May 5, 1980, the Iranian Embassy siege ended after SAS commandoes stormed the building rescuing the hostages. BBC sound recordist Sim Harris, one of the British hostages, scrambled to safety as flames billow from the window. Two explosions heralded the attack that ended the six-day siege at the building in Princes Gate, London.

Left: A car bomb planted by the IRA kills five people outside the Harrods store in London. The remains of the Austin 1100 used in the car bomb attack is seen in Hans Crescent, December 17, 1983.

Right: The Cenotaph at Enniskillen with the devastated community center in the background. 11 people died and more than 50 were injured in a massive IRA bomb explosion just before a Remembrance Day ceremony took place in the Co. Fermanagh town of Enniskillen, Northern Ireland, November 9, 1987.

Far Right: A policeman walks in front of the cockpit debris of the Pan Am Boeing 747, December 21, 1988, a day after it blew up in flight over Lockerbie, Scotland, killing 258 people on board. The US, Britain, and Libya are close to reaching an agreement on a multibillion-dollar compensation deal for the relatives of victims of the bombing.

Right: The shattered top four floors of Grand Hotel, Brighton, which was devastated by an IRA bomb that left five people dead and 31 injured during the 1984 Conservative Party Conference, October 12, 1984.

Right: A picture of the end of the Waco siege as the Branch Davidian cult compound observation tower is engulfed in flames. The fire is suspected to have been started from inside the compound after it was alleged that federal agents began pumping tear gas into the building.

Below: An aerial view of the Italian cruise ship *Achille Lauro* on fire in the Indian Ocean off the coast of Somalia taken from a US Navy helicopter. Passengers were rescued from lifeboats by ships in the area. Several people are reported to have died. Launched as the *Willem Ruys* in 1947, named *Achille Lauro* in 1964, this ship did not have a charmed life. After suffering serious fires in 1965 and 1972, in 1975 it collided with a livestock carrier. In December 1981 three passengers were killed after another fire, but the most notorious incident was when, in October 1985, a Palestinian group hijacked the liner and murdered an American passenger. The ship went to a watery grave on December 2, 1994, while under tow by a salvage vessel.

Right: Passengers wait to receive medical attention after Aum cult terrorists release Sarin nerve gas into Tokyo subway trains. 12 killed and 5,000 injured. March 20, 1995.

Below: The Albert P. Murrah Federal Building in Oklahoma City and the devastation caused by a fuel-and fertilizer truck bomb that was detonated early April 19, 1995, in front of the building. The blast, the worst terror attack on US soil at the time, killed 168 people. Timothy McVeigh, convicted on first-degree murder charges for the April 19 bombing is scheduled to be executed.

Above: Federal agents sift through the rubble at the base of the sound stack in Centennial Park, Atlanta, where a bomb exploded July 27, 1996. Two people were killed in the blast.

Right: Smoke rises on August 7, 1998, from the site of a huge explosion that shook a bank building and the US embassy in central Nairobi killing at least 60 people and leaving more than 1,000 injured. The explosion was caused by a bomb. US ambassador Prudence Bushnell was slightly hurt in the blast.

TERRORISM

Left: Indonesian Agus Dwikarna, who was sentenced to 17 years in jail in the Philippines for illegal possession of explosives, attends a courtroom hearing in Manila August, 23, 2002, for a motion for reconsideration, seeking his acquittal. Dwikarna charged that he had been set up in the explosives conviction and denied accusations by Philippine officials that he was involved with terrorist groups like the Jemaah Islamiya or al-Qaeda. Philippine officials allege that Dwikarna had also been implicated in bombing attacks that claimed over a dozen lives in Manila in December 2000 and in a bomb attack on the Philippine embassy in Indonesia in the same year.

Below: The damage to USS *Cole* in the Yemeni port of Aden following a terrorist attack on October 12, 2000.

Above: Police officers stand behind a cordon following a suspected car bomb explosion near Ealing Broadway station in West London, March 3, 2001.

Right: People standing in front of a bomb-destroyed bank branch in central Madrid, Thursday, June 28, 2001. The blast was blamed on the Basque separatist group ETA. It injured at least 14 people, including a retired Spanish army general who seems to have been the target of the attack. In its 33-year terror campaign, ETA—whose aim is to establish an independent Basque state in northeastern Spain and southwestern France—has killed around 800 people.

TERRORISM

Above: A view to the damaged apartment where Olaia Castresana, an alleged member of Basque separatist organization ETA, died when an explosive device she was manipulating exploded late Tuesday, July 24, 2001. Seven other people were injured in the blast.

Below: CCTV photographs released by Scotland Yard showing a car bomb explosion that injured 11 people in Ealing, West London, just after midnight, August 3, 2001.

TERRORISM

Above: September 11, 2001—workers watch smoke billow from the Pentagon in Washington.

Left: Smoke billows from the World Trade Center.

Right: One of the towers begins to collapse.

TERRORISM

Left: View of smoke billowing from the Madrid-Barajas airport parking lot where a booby-trapped car exploded on Monday, August 27, 2001. Nobody was injured in the blast which occurred shortly after police received a telephone warning from a caller saying he represented the Basque separatist group ETA. A spokesman said up to 60 vehicles in the second floor of the airport's terminal 2 building were damaged in the blast which also started a fire.

Left and Above Left: Two more photos of the 9-11 outrage. The top picture shows the moment of the second impact. The bottom photo is an aerial view looking north from southern Manhattan as smoke rises from the ruins of the World Trade Center.

Right: Philippines special action forces armed with assault rifles escort alleged Indonesian terror suspects, Agus Dwikarna (2nd R) and Tamsil Linrung (Center back with white shirt) during a court appearance in Manila, April 3, 2002. The two men were arrested at a Manila airport March 13 after police said they found bomb-making materials in their bags as they were about to fly to Thailand.

Left: Inside a courtroom in Rotterdam in December 2002 an artist sketches four men accused of being members of a Europe-wide Islamic extremist network that plotted attacks on US targets on the continent. It is the first time since the September 11 terror attacks on the US that suspected Islamic militants have gone on trial before a Dutch court.

Right: Thousands take to the streets of Bilbao during a protest rally against Basque separatist terror called by the Basque Country's regional President Juan Jose Ibarretxe, Sunday, December 22, 2002. The slogan on the placard in Basque reads "ETA out."

Below: Chechen rebels take 763 hostages in Moscow theater; after tense days negotiating Russian authorities release a gas into the theater, killing 116 hostages and freeing the remainder October 26, 2002.

Above: Injured British tourist James Woodley walks amongst the debris in Kuta Beach after the November 2002 weekend's bombing of two popular bars in which almost 190 people were killed, many of them Australians.

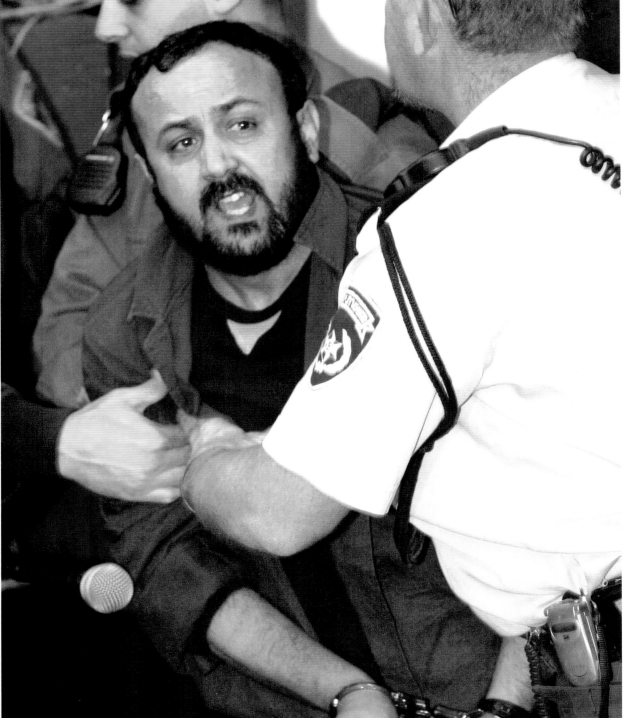

Left: Marwan Barghuti, the West Bank leader of Palestinian leader Yasser Arafat's Fatah movement, is brought into the Tel Aviv district court January 2, 2003. Barghuti, once tipped as a possible successor to Arafat, was captured in April 2002 and was charged with various counts of murder and "heading a terrorist organization." He is as perfect an example of the dictum "one man's terrorist is another's freedom fighter" as any man with a cause.

Right: Singaporean Mas Selamat bin Kastari, is guarded by Indonesian police in Tanjung Pinang on Bintang island, Riau, February 4, 2003. A leading member of the Jemaah Islamiyah regional network he had allegedly plotted to crash a hijacked plane in Singapore.

Below: Ali Imron (L), one of the key suspects of Bali bombing, explains how the bombs were assembled while two policemen dressed as accomplices (C and R) assist during a press conference at police headquarters in Bali, February 11, 2003. The key suspect Ali Imron publicly admitted his role in the Bali terror blasts and gave details of how the deadly attacks were carried out.

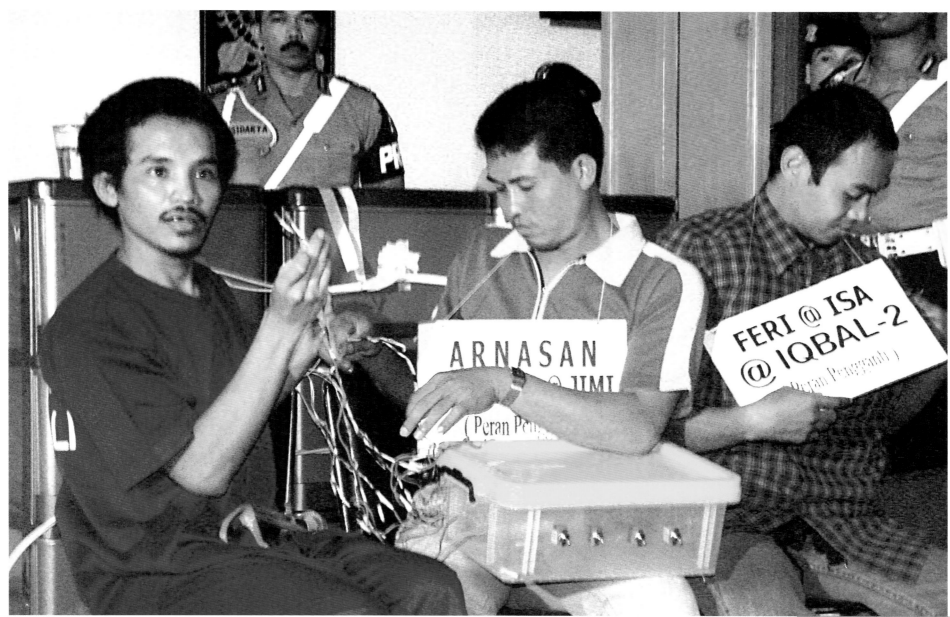

Left: A British soldier talks on his radio while patrolling Terminal 4 at London's Heathrow airport, Friday February 14, 2003. Seven people have been arrested overnight under the terrorist laws in the area around Heathrow and a Venezuelan man was caught with a hand grenade in his luggage at London's Gatwick airport. The Army continue their patrols at Britain's largest airport after being drafted in by Prime Minister Tony Blair to respond to intelligence reports on possible terror attacks. However, it was alleged in the aftermath of the Gulf War that the military presence had more to do with public opinion than a real terrorist threat. Certainly, the grenade found at Gatwick was not a terrorist tool.

Below: French Judicial Police investigate the scene of the bomb blast at the Farah Hotel in Casablanca, Sunday, May 18, 2003. This was the scene of one of five simultaneous suicide bombings that claimed 40 lives in the seaside city of Casablanca in Morocco late Friday May 16.

TERRORISM

Left: The price of freedom is vigilance—Indonesian Mobile Brigade policemen pointing their rifles to an unidentified man during an antiterror simulation at Jakarta's police headquarters, May 19, 2003, a few hours after the Indonesian government declared martial law in Aceh.

Below: A US Navy security boat carrying armed soldiers patrols the waters near a docked submarine on the west side of Manhattan along the Hudson River May 23, 2003, in New York City. The US Coast Guard faced a triple challenge that weekend with the heightened terror alert, Fleet Week, and the kick-off of the Memorial Day weekend for boaters.

Above: Hundreds of Shi'ite Muslim students fill the streets of Lahore and burn tires during a mourning ceremony on Saturday, June 5, 2003. Three suicide bombers died during an attack on a packed mosque in Quetta yesterday during the Friday prayers and left 47 people killed and some 50 injured. Tensions between Shi'ites and majority Sunni Muslims were severely strained.

Left: The Imam of the Gallarate, Milan mosque Mohamed El Mahfoudi, of Agadir, Morocco, arrested by Italian police in Milan, June 24, 2003. The cleric and five other men are suspected of financing an Islamic extremist organization that has links to Osama bin Laden's al Qaeda group.

TERRORISM

Right: Alleged Indonesian terrorist Fathur Rohman al Ghozi (2nd from L) is escorted to a Manila court Wednesday, July 2, 2003, before being questioned for his involvement in a bombing in December 2000 of a train station which killed more than 20 passengers and injured hundreds.

Below: Police specialists inspect the bodies of the victims at the site of explosions on Tushino airfield near Moscow, Saturday, July 5, 2003. At least 17 people were killed and 20 heavily injured as a result of two explosions during a rock concert. Police blame the blasts on Chechen women suicide bombers.

1902
Mount Pelée erupts on Saint Pierre Martinique—30,000 die.

1903
Chicago fire in Iroquois Theatre kills 602.

1904
Blaze spreads through downtown Baltimore. More than 1,500 buildings were destroyed. Damages $150 million, but no lives lost.

1905
Earthquake in Kashmir kills 19,000.

1906
Earthquake in San Francisco kills 667.
Mt. Vesuvius erupts.
Earthquake in Valparaiso, Chile kills 20,000.

1908
Earthquake in Messina, Sicily kills 75,000.

1912
Titanic strikes an iceberg in the Atlantic—1,523 dead.
Explosion levels part of Halifax and kills 1,600 people.

1914
Eruption of Lassen Peak, Northeastern California

1915
Earthquake in Avezzano, Italy kills 30-39,000.

1918
Spanish Flu kills over 20 million people worldwide.

1920
Earthquake in Kansu, China kills 180,000+.

1921
Famine in Russia hits at least 32 million.

1922
Typhoon hits Shantou—28,000 die.

1923
Earthquake in Tokyo & Yokohama kills 143,000

1927
Earthquake in Nan-Shan, China kills 200,000.

1931
Yellow River, China, floods—3,700,000 dead.

1932–39
7,465,000 die of hunger in famine caused by Stalin.

1932
Earthquake in Gansu, China—70,000 killed.

1934–53
Up to 15 million Russians disappeared in the Gulags.

1935
Earthquake in Quetta, India–30-50,000 die.

1937
New London, Tex.: explosion destroys school; 294 killed.

1934–45
Over 6 million Jews and 5 million non-Jews die in German camps, mainly Polish Christians and Catholics.

1940
Lancastria (Cunard/Military troopship): sunk by German bomber, off St. Nazaire 3,500-6,500 killed.

1943
Bengal: 1,500,000 died of war-related famine.
Eruption of Paricutin, Mexico.

1944
Toyama Maru (Japanese Navy transport) sunk by torpedoes from sub USS Sturgeon; 5,400 killed.

1945
East Prussia: up to 3 million German civilians were killed by Russians in the last months of WWII.
Wilhelm Gustloff (German refugee ship)sunk by torpedoes from Soviet sub S-13; 6,000 to 8,000 die.

1947
Most of Texas City destroyed by a fire and subsequent explosion on the French freighter Grandcamp, which was carrying a cargo of ammonium nitrate. At least 516 were killed and over 3,000 injured.

1949
Earthquake in Tazhikistan, USSR: 120,000 die.

1950
Earthquake in Assam, India: 20-30,000 die.

1957
Asian flu kills about 69,800 people in the US.

1960
Earthquake in Agadir, Morocco: 10-20,000 die.

Natural disasters occurred as regularly as usual throughout the 20th century—earthquakes, hurricanes, volcanoes, tidal waves, freezing weather, scorching temperatures, disease—leaving disaster in its wake. But advances in technology have also contributed to the tally of disasters.

The worst volcanic eruption of the century was the third worst in recorded history. Around 40,000 people died when the previously dormant volcano Mont Pelée on the tiny island of Martinique suddenly exploded on May 8, 1902. The sheer number of active volcanoes on earth—over 600—and the richness of the soil on their slopes ensure that man often lives too close for comfort.

There is no doubt that the largest losses of life caused by natural disasters are those caused by earthquakes, particularly those in remote regions without the emergency services of modern Japan or California, whose long involvement with plate tectonics has given a degree of efficiency in their response. Earthquake-aware architecture, emergency facilities, and modern communications all help—unlike the first major earthquake of the century. It occurred under Messina in Italy on December 28, 1908 when about 160,000 people were killed and many more injured. The worst earthquake of the century struck at Tang-shan in China on July 28, 1976 when the devastation left 242,419 people dead or missing. Worse than the death toll caused by the San Francisco earthquake in April 1906 were the estimated 700 deaths in the fires following the quake.

With the increasing population of the planet it is inevitable that disease and epidemics can decimate entire areas. Just at the beginning of World War One (1914–15) a typhus epidemic in Eastern Europe accounted for around 3,000,000 people. Then, a few years later in 1918–20 an influenza epidemic swept around the world infecting millions and killing an estimated 21,640,000—more than the war itself had managed. The current AIDS epidemic is the world's single greatest health disaster and affects people in virtually every country on the planet. So far estimates suggest that over 12,000,000 men, women,

DISASTERS

and children have died, although many millions more are affected. The panic that accompanied the SARS virus indicates how dangerous these pandemics are.

Man-made disasters are usually on a much smaller scale. The manufacture of chemicals is particularly hazardous. In May 1918 at Oakdale in America a chemical explosion killed 193 people. However, the century's worst commercial disaster occurred at the Union Carbide plant at Bhopal, India on December 3, 1984. No one knows for sure how many people died when the lethal gas Methyl isocyanate escaped but it was probably around 3,000.

Explosions also account for many deaths and injuries: one of the worst was in Afghanistan in the Salang Tunnel in November 1982 when a gasoline tanker collision caused the death of over 2,000 people. Mining is another very dangerous occupation and accounts for a regular death tally. But the very nature of the business means that the scale of mining disasters are relatively easy to disguise. For example, it is believed that up to 3,000 people may have died in a disaster at the Fushun mines in Manchuria in February 1931 but the details were hushed up. Similarly mining disasters in East Germany and South Africa have been hushed up so the mortality details will never be known. One of the most tragic disasters was the deaths of 116 schoolchildren in their little school in the mining town of Aberfan, Wales. During the day of October 20, 1966 the 800ft water-sodden slag heap slid down the hill and engulfed the school.

Systems of transportation can often lead to horrific disasters. Shipwrecks, air crashes, railroad accidents, freeway pileups: the century abounds with examples of these tragedies. However, other man-made disasters kill more substantial numbers: the killing fields of Pol Pot, Hitler's camps, and the appalling results of Stalin's purges were responsible for more deaths and suffering than anything except the great pandemics.

1963
USS *Thresher* (USN submarine) sinks after electrical failure, North Atlantic: 129 die.
Volcano erupts in Bali, killing 11,000.

1964
Tsunami at Prince William's Sound, Alaska.
Lima, Peru: more than 300 soccer fans killed and over 500 injured after controversial refereeing decision.

1966
Aberfan disaster kills 144 including 116 schoolchildren.

1967
Oil tanker Torrey Canyon wrecked off Britain's south coast: Ecological disaster.

1968
Earthquake in NE Iran kills 12,000.
Hong Kong Flu kills 33,800—the mildest pandemic in the 20th century.

1970
Earthquake in Yunnan, China kills 10,000.
Earthquake in NW Peru kills 50-67,000

1975
Edmund Fitzgerald sinks during storm on Lake Superior: 29 die.

1975–79
In Cambodia, Khmer Rouge's Pol Pot kills nearly two million of his own people.

1976
Earthquake in Guatemala, 23,000 die.

1977
Two Boeing 747s collide on runway at Tenerife: 583 die.

1978
Abadan, Iran: nearly 400 killed when arsonists set fire to crowded theater.
Earthquake in Tabas, NE Iran. 25,000

1978
Eruption of Mount Saint Helens, Washington

1983
Soviets shoot down Korean Air Lines 747 over Sakhalin Island: 269 die.

1984
Bhopal, India, a Union Carbide plant burns, 6,500 die.

1985
Bradford, England: 56 burned to death and over 200 injured when fire engulfs soccer stadium.
Japan Airlines 747 crashes into Mt. Otsuka: 520 die.
Earthquake in Mexico. between 5 and 25,000 die.
Earthquake in Colombia follows Nevado del Ruiz's eruption—25,000 die in mudflows.

1985
Chernobyl nuclear reactor meltdown kills 31 but spreads contamination all over Europe.
Dona Paz is in collision with oil tanker Victor in the Tablas Strait. There are 4,341 deaths.

1988
Earthquake in Armenia. 25-55,000 die.
USS *Vincennes* shoots down Iran Air Airbus: 290 die.

1990
Earthquake in NW Iran kills 35-50,000.

1991
Eruption of Mt. Pinatubo, Luzon, Philippines.
Eruption of Cerro Hudson, Chile.

1993
Bangkok, Thailand: fire in doll factory killed at least 187 persons and injured 500 others. World's deadliest factory fire.

1993–94
Estonia swamped through bow door and sank in Baltic Sea killing 1,049.

1995
Earthquake in Kobe, Japan kills 6,500.

2000
Kursk (Russian submarine) sunk by internal explosion or collision, Barents Sea
Earthquake in Golkar, NW Turkey kills 45,000.
Cable car transporting skiers to the Kitzsteinhorn glacier broke into flames: 156 die.
Earthquake in Gujarat, NW India, kill 20.000+.

2003
SARS virus spreads rapidly from China, but swift quarantine limits outbreaks.

Above: Smoke coming from a cone within the crater of Vesuvius. This volcano would erupt a number of times in the 20th century including 1944 as the Allies fought the Germans.

Above Left: A photograph c1912 of the "unsinkable" *Titanic*, which sank off Newfoundland on her maiden voyage to the US after striking an iceberg; 1513 people lost their lives.

Left: A view of one of the outlying districts of Tokyo after the earthquake of September 1, 1923.

Right: The German airship *Hindenburg*, sporting swastika flags on her tail fins, flying over the 1936 Berlin Olympic Games. On May 6, 1937, the airship exploded in a ball of fire as she came in to land in Lakehurst NAS, New Jersey. At least 33 passengers and crew were killed. The crash was witnessed by radio commentator Herb Morrison of WLS Radio who broadcast a live coverage of the tragedy. The event effectively killed off the use of airships as a method of mass transit. On a lighter note, the image of the burning zeppelin was used to great effect on the cover of Led Zeppelin's first album.

Above: Photo dated August 8, 1956, of the fire in the coal mine Bois du Cazier in Marcinelle, France, in which 268 miners died.

Above Left: War provides some of the biggest disasters. For the 60th Anniversary of the Japanese attack, the US Marines Corps released some never seen before pictures. of Pearl Harbor. Here one of many of NAS Kaneohe Bay's planes burns in the bay after the December 7, 1941, attack.

Left: Rescue workers searching through the wreckage for dead and injured passengers after an express train hit the rear of a local train at Harrow and Wealdstone station in Middlesex in October 1952.

Right: Soldiers and miners at work amid the wreckage after a coal tip slid down the mountain and buried children in Pantglas Junior School in the South Wales mining village of Aberfan, October 20, 1966. 116 children and 28 adults lost their lives in the disaster. A pile of shovels can be seen in the foreground.

Left: This October 28, 2002, photo shows the continuing eruption of Europe's largest and most active volcano, Mt. Etna, on the island of Sicily. A dense plume of what is likely to be ash and smoke is streaming southward from the volcano and out over the Mediterranean Sea.

Below: On June 18, 1972, a BEA Trident crashed in a field in Staines killing all 118 people on board. This photograph shows an engine nacelle still intact on the tail section of the Brussels-bound aircraft. The fuselage (background) ploughed on into a line of trees.

Above: A snow-clearer digs his way through the snow in Schleswig-Holstein on January 2, 1979. After a six-day snow disaster the roads were once more drivable again. More than a thousand Bundeswehr soldiers, police, and other relief organizations had been in action to help the cut-off villages in northern Germany.

Right: This image was taken on August 22, 1999, by NASA's Landsat 7 satellite. It shows Mt. St. Helens as it looks 20 years after the catastrophic eruption of the volcano. The height of Mt. St. Helens was reduced from 9,677ft to about 8,364ft in the eruption on the morning of May 18, 1980. A column of dust and ash more than 25 km (15.5 miles) into the atmosphere and shock waves from the blast knocked down trees within five miles of the central crater.

Left: Bradford City's Valley Parade football ground burns on May 11, 1985. *T*he inferno claimed the lives of 56 football fans and injured hundreds of others.

Below: A photograph taken January 28, 1986, shows the two solid fuel rocket boosters flaring away from the explosion of the space shuttle *Challenger*. The shuttle, carrying seven crew members, including teacher Christa McAuliffe, exploded 75 seconds after its launch and killed all crew members.

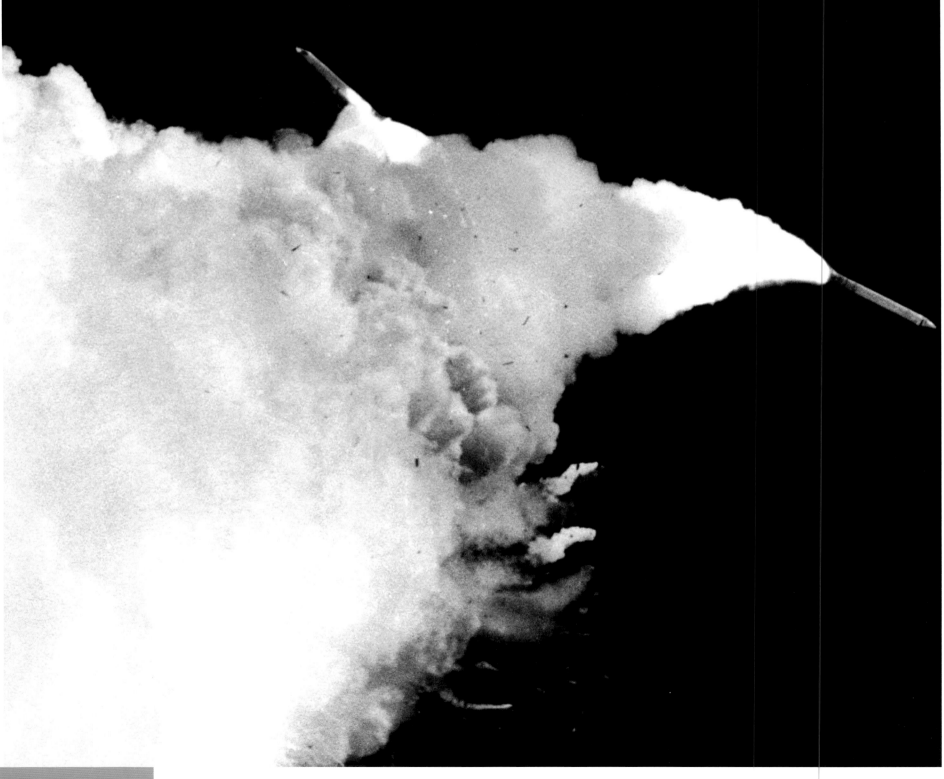

DISASTERS

Left: The damaged unit number 4 at Chernobyl nuclear power plant in the Ukraine, USSR, after the disaster. While the immediate death toll was limited, long-term deaths due to radiation-related illnesses such as cancers and leukemia are bound to be significant. The radioactive plume from Chernobyl meant that fallout affected livestock as far away as Scotland and Wales.

Below: On March 6, 1987, the Townsend Thorensen car ferry *Herald of Free Enterprise* capsized outside Zeebrugge harbor, Belgium. 194 people, including 38 crew, lost their lives when the ferry capsized after starting its journey with the bow doors were left open.

Left: Tributes at Hillsborough, remembering those who died at the disaster during an FA Cup semi-final soccer match between Liverpool and Nottingham Forest on April 13, 1999. 96 people died and 170 were injured.

Below: On January 18, 1995, a killer earthquake hit Japan. The city of Kobe in the Kansai region was hardest hit. The quake measured 7.2 on the Richter scale, destroying houses, expressways, and bridges. The damage would have been even greater had the Japanese not built with the possibility of earthquakes in mind. The death toll, nevertheless, reached 6,500.

Right: The flowers massed at the gates of Dunblane Primary School, March 14, 1996. The day before a lone gunman, Thomas Hamilton, killed 16 children—all aged around five or six—and a teacher in a random attack in the school gym. Twelve other children were taken to hospital where another died. Hamilton then killed himself.

Below: The reconstructed fuselage of TWA Boeing 747 flight 800 on display in Calverton, Maryland. An accidental explosion inside a fuel tank caused the aircraft to explode in midair in July 1996, killing 230 on board. US investigators probing the midair explosion of the flight found no proof criminal activity was behind the disaster.

Left: A massive column of smoke billows over the Soufrière Hills volcano as it erupted again on August 8, 1997. Guadeloupe and other islands worked on a plan for the possible evacuation of the 5,000 people on the British Caribbean colony. The plan was necessary: when the volcano started venting poisonous gasses it was time for the islanders to leave.

Below: On June 3, 1998, an inter-city ICE express train from Munich to Hamburg slammed into a bridge in the town of Eschede at a speed of 200km/hr (125mph). 101 people died and 105 were injured in Eschede near the northern city of Celle.

DISASTERS

Above: A neighborhood in Armenia, Colombia, lies in ruin after the city—200 miles west of Bogota—was rocked by an earthquake on January 25, 1999. The earthquake, which measured six on the Richter scale, killed more than 500 people and left hundreds more injured and homeless.

Right: An aerial view of Tungshih, Taiwan, after the island was hit by its strongest earthquake this century on September 21, 1999. At least 1,546 people were killed and 3,841 people injured when the quake struck, measuring up to 8.1 on the Richter scale.

Left: A woman carries drinking water and food back to her house after wading through chest high flood waters on October 5, 1999 in Ranaghat, West Bengal. Some three million people were affected by floods in the area.

Below: The Ecuadoran volcano Tungurahua continues to spew smoke and ash on October 23, 1999. The volcano ejected red-glowing incandescent rocks 22 October, a sign that experts say indicates the mount is about to erupt. They were correct! In November and December 1999 Tungurahua extruded lava in a series of explosive events culminating in a major eruption on November 4. Activity continues today.

Above: Aerial view on Sunday, November 14, 1999, showing the damage in the northwestern Turkish town of Duzce after an earthquake measuring 7.2 on the Richter scale hit the region. At least 347 people were killed and 2,923 injured in the quake.

Right: A view taken on the morning of January 5, 2000, of crashed wagons and the rear-engine of one of the two trains that collided head-on near Rena, close to the former Winter Olympics town of Lillehammer in Norway, claiming at least seven lives.

Right: Lava explodes from the crater of Mayon volcano spewing out vast clouds of superhot ash and molten rocks during its eruption early February 24, 2000, in the eastern Philippine province of Albay. About 4,000 people were evacuated from the areas surrounding the volcano which sent a cloud of ash and rocks rolling down its slopes. Mayon had been showing signs of renewed activity for months prior to its eruption.

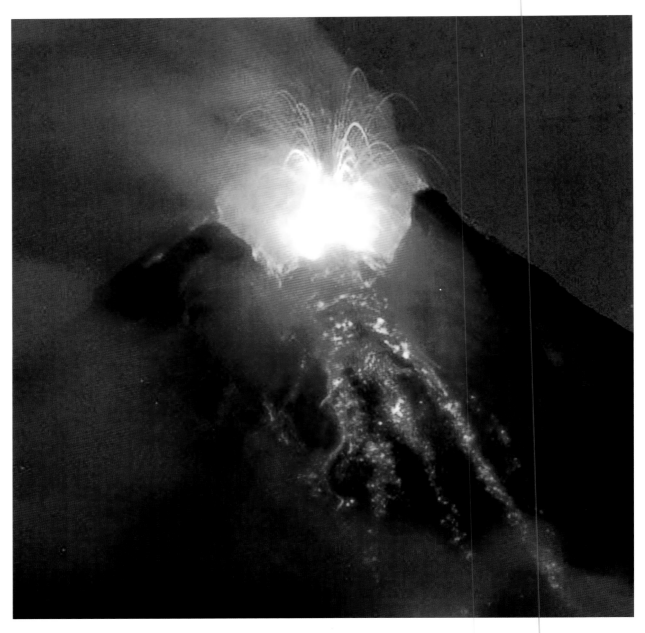

Below: The Russian submarine *Kursk* at her mooring in the base of Vidyayevo. On August 14, 2000, the Russian Navy identified a problem with the submarine—while on exercises in the Barents Sea, it had sunk to the seafloor and the lives of the 118 crew were threatened. As the story unfolded it became clear that an internal explosion had sunk the Kursk, but that some of the crew survived until they succumbed to cold and lack of oxygen. The submarine was raised on October 11, 2001, and a memorial plaque was left on the seabed.

Above: Rescue workers search around the tail section of smoldering wreckage from the Air Philippines plane crash on Samal Island, April 19, 2000. It killed all 131 on board in the country's worst aviation disaster. The burning wreckage of the Boeing 737-200 was found on the nearby Samal Island soon after the pilot aborted his final approach to the southern city of Davao on seeing another aircraft on the runway, airport authorities said.

Right: The crumpled remains of a large home in the town of Cubuk, north of Ankara, Turkey early Tuesday June 6, 2000, following an earthquake that measured 5.9 on the Richter scale.

Right: Debris of the Concorde landing gear on the site of the accident in Gonesse, outside Paris. The Air France Concorde that crashed on July 25, 2000, killing 113 people had multiple problems during its takeoff before the disaster, France's Accident Investigation Bureau (BEA) revealed on Thursday, July 27. Bits of tire were left behind as the supersonic jet roared down the runway with one wing in flames, both port engines suffered troubles and the landing carriage would not retract, the BEA said in a statement.

Below: Smoke rises from Mount Oyama volcano on Miyakejima island, August 10, 2000. Japanese authorities evacuated families after ash rained down on their homes in the island's northeast. Mount Oyama had resumed activity on July and it erupted on August 18, sending rocks and smoke over 20,000ft into the sky.

DISASTERS

Left: A pyroclastic flow from Mount Oyama, some 125 miles south of Tokyo, heads into the sea in the early morning of August 29, 2000. With clouds of smoke reaching five miles in height, all inhabitants were evacuated.

Below: An aerial view taken on Tuesday, October 17, 2000,showing the damage caused by floods in the area between the villages of Fenis and Nus in the Italian northernwestern region Valle d'Aosta. Thirteen persons were reported dead, 18 missing and some 25,000 were evacuated following bad weather which hit three Italian northernwestern regions. Italian government decreed state of emergency on Monday in the regions Piemonte, Valle d' Aosta and Liguria.

Right: Passers-by look at a destroyed building where they used live in the town of Bhuj, in Gujarat state, which along with the entire northwestern India was hit by a massive earthquake on January 26, 2001. An estimated 20,000 people are thought to have been killed in the quake, the worst to hit India for 50 years.

Below: Giant plumes of black smoke billow from a slum housing area in downtown Phnom Penh, as a massive fire engulfs the wooden houses built on the roof of a run-down housing estate. According to first police reports, some 235 houses were destroyed on March 12, 2002, with no immediate reports of deaths but there were fears some of the estimated 1,000 people who lived in the affected area could have been trapped in the three hours it took firefighters to bring the blaze under control.

Above: Crash investigators at the scene of a rail crash at Potter's Bar station, Hertfordshire. Seven people are now reported dead from the derailment which took place on May 10, 2002. More information as to the cause of the crash was released in a report on the accident from the Health and Safety Executive. The report threw more light on the state of the set of points at the center of the investigation.

Right: This dreadful photograph shows an SU-27 crashing during an air show in Lviv, Ukraine, on July 29, 2002. The world's worst airshow crash saw 199 people injured and 83 died including 15 children. More than 1,000 Ukrainians gathered at the airfield to attend a memorial service for those who died and were injured in the weekend air show disaster.

Above: Partly destroyed houses and cars buried under the debris in Schlans, a village in Graubuenden, eastern Switzerland, Sunday, November 17, 2002. A mudslide set off by heavy rain injured several people and damaged parts of Schlans. The mudslide went right through the middle of the village and hit some houses, according to the cantonal police.

Below: This aerial view shows the flooded city center of Dresden in the German state of Saxony. Heavy rainfalls in Germany, Austria, Czech Republic and Poland caused a disastrous flood in central Europe.

Above: Aerial photo dated December 15, 2002, showing the Norwegian car-carrier *Tricolor*, lying on its side at low tide in the English Channel some 10 miles off the French coast, after colliding with the Bahamas container ship *Kariba*. A tanker, the *Vicky*, carrying 70,000 tons of highly flammable gas oil, struck the submerged hull January 1, 2003, according to British coastguards. The French coastguard was coordinating a rescue operation for the crew of the tanker which was said to have become stuck in the wreck, it was reported.

Below: Rescuers try to free a trapped man after a crane collapsed at the construction site of a 100-story financial center following a powerful earthquake in Taipei March 31, 2002.

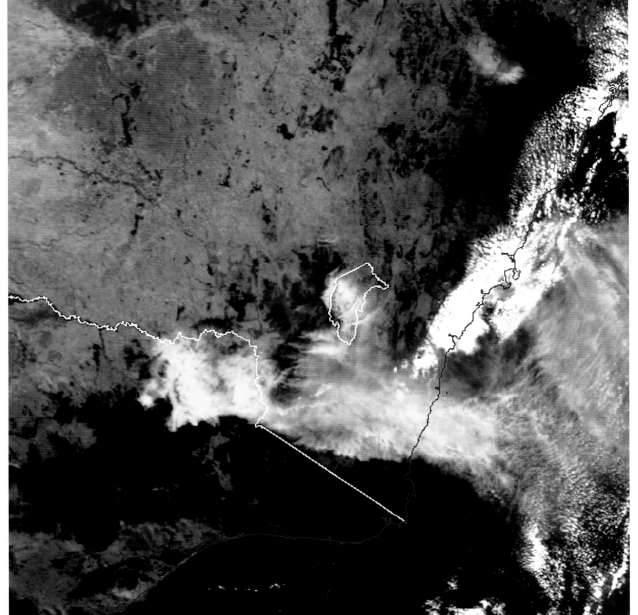

Above: A bird's eye view of the once lush island of Anuta in the Solomon Islands which was devastated by cyclone Zoe. It appears stripped clean of vegetation during a French Defence Force reconnaissance flight, January 2003. Zoe, rated category five and packing winds in excess of 300 km/h, caused widespread damage to subsistence crops, coconut palms and breadfruit trees when it hit the island last weekend while the extent of casualties is still not known.

Right: Emergency services attend the scene of a commuter train derailment in bushland near Waterfall, south of Sydney, January 2003. At least eight people were killed and dozens injured after the train carrying 80 people derailed.

Left: This satellite image of January 18, 2003, shows smoke from bushfires across southeast Australia, including the ones that devastated the capital Canberra in the Australian Capital Territory (ACT). ACT emergency services were expecting weather conditions next weekend similar to those that created fires January 18-19, that claimed four lives and destroyed 419 homes.

Right: February 21, 2003—Mexico's Popocatepetl volcano spews smoke and ash over the city of Puebla 35 miles southeast of the Mexican capital. Popocatepetl, nicknamed "Don Goyo," is one of the most active volcanoes in the Americas. Before February 2003, it last underwent a period of violent activity in December 2000, forcing the evacuation of thousands of people who make their homes near its base.

Far Right: Rescuers on the scene of a massive pileup which happened on a northern Italian highway shrouded in thick fog on March 13, 2003. About a hundred cars and trucks collided on the highway that runs between the north eastern cities of Trieste and Venice. At least 14 people were killed and 85 remained injured in the crash.

Below: Overall view of what remained of The Station night club in West Warwick, Rhode Island, February 23, 2003. A fire razed it to the ground killing 96 people and sending hundreds more to the hospital. Pyrotechnics set off by the band Great White started the fire.

They died in the year they would turn:

16

Anne Frank 1929–45. Wartime diarist. Died in Nazi concentration camp.

Died age 18

Ritchie Valens 1941–59. Singer. In a plane crash.

Died age 21

Stuart Sutcliffe 1940–1962. Early Beatle. Brain hemorrhage.

Died age 22

Eddie Cochran 1938–1960. Singer. Car wreck.

Lilian Board 1958 –1970. Athlete/runner. Cancer.

Aaliyah Dana Haughton 1979–2001. Singer. Plane crash.

Sid Vicious 1957–1979. Punk. Heroin overdose.

Died age 23

Buddy Holly 1936–59. Singer/songwriter/musician. Plane crash.

River Phoenix 1970–1993. Movie actor. Overdose of heroin and cocaine.

Violet Szabo 1921–1945. British S.O.E. spy. Shot at Ravensbruck concentration camp.

Died age 24

James Dean 1931–55. Film actor/icon. In a car crash.
Selena Quintanilla 1971–1995. Singer. Shot in back.

Died age 25

Wilfred Owen 1893–1918. Poet. Killed in action, France.
Tupac Shakur 1971–1996. Rapper. Gunned in Las Vegas.

Died age 26

Guy Gibson 1918–44. Pilot/ Dambusters. Killed on later operation.

Jean Harlow 1911–37. Movie actress. Cerebral oedema.

Sharon Tate 1943–1969. Movie actress. Murdered by Charles Manson and The Family.

Died age 27

Kurt Cobain 1967–94. Singer/songwriter/musician with Nirvana. Suicide with a shotgun.

Bryan Jones 1942–1969. Musician/Rolling Stone. Excess, drowning.

Janis Joplin 1943–70. Singer. Accidental overdose.

Died age 28

Bix Beiderbecke. 1903–31. Jazz cornettist. Pneumonia following alcoholism.

Rupert Brooke 1887–1915. Poet. Of dysentry on Skyros.

Piers Courage 1942–1970. F1 driver. Crash at Zandvoort.

Jimi Hendrix 1942–70. Singer/musician/composer. Overdose of barbiturates and alcohol.

Brandon Lee 1965–1993. Martial arts movie star. Shooting accident on set.

Jim Morrison 1943–71. Poet/singer with the Doors. Of general excess, in Paris.

Jochen Rindt 1942–1970. F1 driver. Crash at Monza.

Died age 29

"Big Bopper" Jiles Ricardson 1930–1959. Singer. Plane crash.

Mary Jo Kopeckne 1940–1969. Democratic campaigner. Drowned following car wreck.

Tommy Simpson 1938–67. Professional cyclist. Heat exhaustion and amphetamines.

Died age 30

Marc Bolan 1947–1977. Singer. Car wreck.

Died age 31

Sandy Denny 1947–1978. Electric folk singer. Brain hemorrhage.

"Mama" Cass Elliot 1943–1974. Singer. Heart failure.

Sylvia Plath 1932–63. Poet. Committed suicide.

Died age 32

Jim Clark 1936–68. F1 racing driver. Crash during practice at Hockenheim.

The poignancy of dying young touches all of us. A young death is always sad, potential nipped off at the bud, all possibilities terminated. But, somehow, it is even sadder when someone who has achieved something remarkable—like Jimi Hendrix—dies, because they are still early in their career and development and their skill could only get better. But would it have done? Who can say whether any given artist had not already produced to their utmost potential and all the rest of their life it would have been downhill. This is the great unanswerable "what if . . ." question. What would Jimi have written and played had he lived? Furthermore, what have we, as his audience, missed because of his early demise?

The obvious early deaths that spring to mind belong to entertainers, the stars who perform and live in the public eye. This is particularly true of rock and rollers—live fast and die young. So many have lived the high life and paid the ultimate price—Janis Joplin, Sid Vicious, Bryan Jones, Jim Morrison—the list is endless and they really have only themselves to blame. They all wanted a good time at any cost and were hell-bent on self destruction—they ignored all those who told them to slow down.

It is frequently said that the greatest career move for someone in the public eye is to die young: this has been proved over and again—when a performer expires the public rush out to buy their work. Would James Dean be as idolized today had he lived to become fat and bald? Perhaps he would be just another aging Hollywood actor making run-of-the mill heist films for an undemanding public. Endless time can be spent in speculation about what might have been, but nothing can be proved: talent is an elusive thing—some people can produce it time and again for years while others have only one great purple patch and never again reach those heights.

Precocious gifts cut off by tragedy are perhaps the saddest of all—the World War 1 poet Wilfred Owen who was killed in action in northern France used words to convey

TOO YOUNG TO DIE

the full horror of war and shaped many peoples opinions about conflict. Another such poet was Rupert Brooke who died of dysentry in Skyros on his way to join the Royal Navy in the Dardanelles. He never got to fight, but his poems of romantic patriotism and longing struck a deep chord with many people.

Sheer bad luck accounts for many early deaths. The first man in space, cosmonaut Yuri Gagarin, was killed in a plane accident and astronaut Gus Grissom was killed in the fire on Apollo I along with his colleagues Chaffee and White. The explosion after take off of the Space Shuttle *Challenger* claimed seven lives, including that of the first teacher chosen to fly into space, Sharon Christa McAucliffe. Diana, Princess of Wales died in a horrible car wreck in a Parisian underpass when her speeding car hit a pillar. With hindsight all these deaths were preventable, but accidents happen, and that is a fact of life whether you are rich or poor, famous or anonymous.

Illness of course takes many an unfulfilled life. The cellist Jacqueline du Pré was in her forties when she died from multiple sclerosis but her scorching talent lives on in recordings. The influential reggae musician Bob Marley died of cancer while at the height of his fame and creativity. Jean Harlow died young from swelling of the brain. A great loss to the scientific world, and perhaps all of us, was of the x-ray crystallographer Rosalind Franklin who won a posthumous Nobel for her work on DNA.

Another significant factor is that of fatal accident caused by a sports injury. Motorbike and racing drivers are the most obvious examples—Ayrton Senna and Jochen Rindt— both of them tragically died in racing cars, the latter during practice and Senna on the race track. Other sports have less obvious dangers but still people die: anyone in contact sports such as boxing is at risk as are ball players of all kinds.

Lawrence Oates 1880–1912. Antarctic explorer. Exposure.

Died age 33

John Belushi 1949–1982 Comedian/movie star. Massive overdose of cocaine and heroin.

Karen Carpenter 1950–1983. Singer. *Anorexia nervosa*.

Sam Cooke 1931–64 Soul/gospel singer. Shot over dispute with a girl.

Brian Epstein 1934–1967 Beatles manager. Barbiturate overdose.

Bruce Lee 1940–1973. Kung Fu movie star. Oedema.

Dinu Lipatti 1917–1950. Rumanian pianist/composer. Of lymphogranulomatosis, a rare form of cancer.

Died age 34

Alma Cogan 1932–1966. Singer. Long cancer illness.

Yuri Gagarin 1934–68. Cosmonaut. Flying accident.

Carole Lombard 1908–42. Movie actress. Air crash.

Jayne Mansfield 1933–1967. Movie actress. Car wreck.

Ayrton Senna. 1960–94. F1 driver. Race crash/Imola.

Died age 36

Bob Marley 1945–81. Reggae singer/songwriter/musician. Of cancer.

Amedeo Modigliani 1884–1920. Painter/sculptor. Of tuberculosis in Paris.

Marilyn Monroe 1926–62. Movie actress. Accidental drugs overdose or murder.

Diana, Princess of Wales 1961–97. Car wreck in Paris.

Died age 38

Rosalind Franklin 1920–58. Crystallographer/DNA scientist. Cancer.

Florence Griffiths-Joyner 1959–1998 Athlete. Heart seizure from probable steroid abuse.

Amy Johnson 1903–41. Pioneer aviatrix. Lost after bailing out over the Thames.

Sharon Christa McAucliffe 1948–1986. Teacher. *Challenger* explosion.

Died age 39

Fanny Cano 1944–1983. Mexican movie star. Plane crash in which 110 died.

Che Guevara 1928–67. Revolutionary. Executed by Bolivian troops.

Fats Waller 1904–43 Blues/jazz musician/composer. Pneumonia.

Died age 40

John Lennon 1940–80. Composer/musician and Beatle. Shot in New York.

Glenn Miller 1904–44. Band leader/trombonist. Lost without trace in a light aircraft.

Otis Spann 1930–1970. Jazz musician. Cancer.

Died age 41

Lenny Bruce 1925–66. Satirist/comedian. Drugs.

"Gus" Grissom 1926–1967. Astronaut. Apollo explosion.

Died age 42

Jacqueline du Pré 1945–87. Musician/cellist. Multiple sclerosis.
Payne Stewart 1957–1999. Golfer. Flying accident.

Died age 43
Robert Kennedy 1925–68. Politician/presidential candidate. Assassinated in California.

Died age 44
Robert Scott 1868–1912. Antarctic explorer. Died of cold and starvation.

Died age 45
Marvin Gaye 1939–84. Soul singer. Shot by his father.

Died age 46
Freddy Mercury 1946–92. Singer with Queen. AIDS.

John F. Kennedy 1917–63. Politician and 35th president of the USA. Assassinated in Dallas.

Died age 47
Jack Kerouac 1922–69. Beat generation novelist/poet. Alcoholism.

Right: Carole Lombard (1908–42) was the hugely popular Paramount studio star of screwball comedies such as *Nothing Sacred* (1937). Her success started as the cameo blond in Max Sennet comedies in the 1920s, then she became a star in her own right in the 1930s. In 1939 she married the greatest movie star of the time—Clark Gable—and tragically died age 34, at the height of her popularity, in a plane crash.

Left: Jean Harlow (1911–37) was the wisecracking, fast-talking blonde of many early Hollywood films. Initially signed to Howard Hughes she made *Platinum Blonde* (1931), a signature role that turned her into a sex symbol. She moved to MGM and made films such as *Red Dust* (1932). A popular commedienne, she died of cerebral oedema and kidney failure at age 26.

Above: The GIs fighting World War II relaxed and swung to the big band music of Glenn Miller (1904–44). His was one of the most popular dance bands of the swing era, characterized by the precise playing that featured a clarinet leading the saxophone section. Their signature tune was *Moonlight Serenade*, but many other popular tunes such as *In The Mood* characterized the swing era. Miller himself played the trombone, although not outstandingly. In 1942 Miller joined the US Army leading a military band—the Glenn Miller Army Air Force Band. His band had been posted to Paris to entertain the troops six months after D-Day. He was the passenger on a small plane that disappeared into fog over the English Channel and he was never seen again.

Right: Cult figure and Hollywood star James Dean (1931–55) died in his own car when it wrecked on September 30, 1955, just before the release of *East of Eden* (1955). He will forever be remembered as the brooding teenager of *Rebel Without a Cause* (1955) which reinforced his image of disaffected youth. His only other starring role was in *Giant* (1956). His career was just taking off when he died but his early death catapulted him into superstardom.

Left: As a Californian Latin-American Ritchie Valens (1941–59) combined rock'n'roll with Mexican-American music with great success. In 1959 he had a huge double sided hit—*Donna* and on the flip side *La Bamba*. He died in the plane crash that also killed Buddy Holly and the Big Bopper on February 3, 1959.

Right: Mary Jo Kopechne (1940–69) died age 29 seven days short of her birthday, early on the morning of July 19, 1962. She was a passenger in an Oldsmobile sedan driven by US Senator Edward Kennedy. They were returning from a party on Chappaquiddick Island near Martha's Vineyard, Massachusetts, when the car plunged off Dyke Bridge and into a shallow pond. The Senator managed to pull himself out of the water but Mary Jo was trapped and drowned. The accident was not reported for 10 hours and the incident effectively finished Edward Kennedy's hopes of becoming president in the 1972 election. Mary Jo had been an aide for Robert Kennedy during his 1968 presidential campaign and was going to do the same for Edward. Kennedy pled guilty to leaving the scene of an accident and lost his driving license for a year.

Right: Sex goddess and screen luminary Marilyn Monroe (1926–62) was 36 when she died. Famously troubled in her personal life and continually resorting to drink and drugs, Monroe was nevertheless a gifted commedienne as she showed in *Some Like it Hot* (1959). She died at home from an overdose of sleeping pills, probably accidentally. Conspiracy theories surround her death—was it suicide or was it murder? Nobody knows for sure. However, the fact remains that while she may not have been the best actress, she became one of the truly great movie stars of all time.

Left: Sam Cooke (1931–64) was one of the most important and influential soul singers. His background was in gospel singing and he brought that heritage to his voice which was a high, pure tenor. Unusually, he not only wrote many of his own songs, such as *You Send Me* (1957), but also controlled his own career by forming his own record, management, and publishing companies. He was killed in a Los Angeles motel shooting incident in a dispute with the manageress over a girl, just as he was on the verge of a new stage of his career.

Left: Che Guevara (1928–67) was born in Argentina, and traveled widely in Latin America, eventually settling in Guatemala. He believed that only violent revolution would end poverty in Latin America and that the US government would always work to destabilize left wing governments. He met Fidel Castro in Mexico and joined his revolutionary cause in 1956. After the Cuban revolution he held several key posts as one of Castro's most trusted aides and as a legend in his own lifetime was one of the revolution's most effective voices. But he was restless for action and left Cuba in 1965 to organize guerrilla fighters in the Congo, and later Bolivia. Captured and shot by the Bolivian army, he immediately achieved international fame and the status of a martyred hero among leftists worldwide.

Right: Innovative and inspirational Jimi Hendrix (1945–70) provided the soundtrack for the late 1960s, but he became one of the great rock and roll tragedies. A former paratrooper, in his early career he played in bands around the southern states of America and then in New York. He was urged to move to London where he found his true expression and fame with the Jimi Hendrix Experience, then the Band of Gypsies. Naturally left-handed he played a restrung right-handed guitar. He made famous appearances at the Monterey Pop Festival (1967) where he stole the show, Woodstock (1969), and the Isle of Wight Festival (1970). His recording successes include *Hey Joe* (1967) and *Purple Haze* (1967). He died on September 18, 1970, in London from an accidental overdose of barbiturates and alcohol. *Voodoo Chile* (1970) was a posthumous hit.

Left: The undisputed king of Kung Fu movies Bruce Lee, properly Lee Hsiao Lung (1940–73), was an exceptionally agile and skilled martial arts expert. Although born in San Francisco he became a child star in Hong Kong. He developed an interest in martial arts and quickly mastered Wing Chun before progressing to develop his own style of Jeet Kune Do. He started a martial arts school in Seattle and soon got minor Hollywood roles. He found fame in the US in the hit TV series *The Green Hornet*, but in Hong Kong the series made him a superstar. Lee went on to make a number of martial arts movies in Hong King including *Return of the Dragon* (1973), *Fist of Fury*(1972), and *Enter the Dragon* (1973). He died after suffering dizziness, blackouts, and headaches, of apparent cerebral edema (swelling of the brain). His funeral ceremony in Hong Kong was attended by over 25,000 people.

Right: The self-proclaimed "star child" Marc Bolan (1947–77) was a diminutive singer and performer of "glam rock." Between 1970-72 he was a teenage pin-up idol with his pretty, androgynous looks, makeup, and mop of curly hair. As a guitarist he played with a number of musicians before forming the flower power duo Tyrannosaurus Rex. In 1970 he went electric and changed the name of the band to T-Rex. They had a number of hits in Britain including *Ride a White Swan* (1970), and *Metal Guru* (1972). When his popularity as a musician waned he made a TV series which showcased famous guests such as David Bowie (see right). He died in a car wreck in southwest London just as filming finished.

Left: John Winston Lennon was born in humble circumstances in Liverpool, England in 1940 and died a wealthy man when he was shot on the streets of Manhattan in 1980. He achieved global fame as one of the Beatles and moved to New York after the band split up, but his radical politics coupled with raucous rock and roll made him enemies in high places who tried to get him deported back to Britain. His final work was the album *Double Fantasy* (1980) that included the song *Starting Over* which was a hit both sides of the Atlantic after his untimely death.

Below: Bob Marley was responsible for making Jamaican reggae music appreciated around the world. His music stemmed from the politics and theology of his Rastafarian beliefs which he also popularised. The album *Natty Dread* (1974) produced the worldwide hit *No Woman No Cry* that brought his music to the attention of a much wider audience. He toured the world with his music but always returned to Jamaica. In September 1980 he collapsed while on tour in America. He was diagnosed with cancer and died eight months later on May 11, 1981, aged 36.

Right: Marvin Gaye epitomised the Motown sound with a string of hits in the 1960s. A prolific composer he penned many memorable songs including the international best seller *I Heard it Through the Grapevine* (1967). Marvin Gaye worked solo as well as in company with others, in total he had more than 60 hits in the US alone. His personal life became a mess after his marriage broke up in the early 1970s and he got into deep trouble with debt and drugs. Addicted to cocaine with all the consequent mood swings, he was shot dead by his strict Pentecostal father on April 1 during an argument. His father was convicted of involuntary manslaughter.

Below: Wholesome middle-of-the-road brother and sister duo The Carpenters was one of the biggest selling recording acts of the 1970s, with a string of hits like *Close To You* (1970) and *For All We Know* (1971). But Karen was badly weakened by *anorexia nervosa* causing a slow-down of their work rate. Despite ceasing recording and treatment, she got worse and died of the disease in Los Angeles in 1983.

Right: Outrageous performer Freddie Mercury lived the hedonist life to the full. He was born Frederick Bulsara in Zanzibar in 1946 and moved to England with his family as a young boy. He joined the band that would shortly become Queen in 1970. Their breakthrough track *Bohemian Rhapsody* (1976) is regularly voted in polls as one of the best songs of all time. Many of Queen's anthemic songs have become sports stadium standards, particularly *We Will Rock You* (1977) and *We Are the Champions* (1977). After embarking on solo projects in the mid 1980s the band were recording together again when it was announced that Freddie Mercury had AIDS. He died November 24, 1991, aged 45. Much of his vast legacy was left for AIDS research.

Below: The founder and inspiration of grunge rock band Nirvana, Curt Cobain was always a deeply troubled man. The band's relatively short recording career started in 1989 with *Bleach* and ended with *In Utero* in 1993; in between came *Nevermind* in 1991, their best selling album. Nirvana's development was hampered by Cobain's serious heroin addiction and was stopped altogether by his suicide in April 1994.

Left: Wreck of Brazilian F1 driver Ayrton Senna's car after its crash at the Imola circuit, San Marino on May 1 1994. His car inexplicably crashed at the Tamburello corner and the team owner Frank Williams and senior aides were charged with manslaughter. Senna was a natural flamboyant driver, he started in karting, then Formula Ford, Formula 3, and then debuted with the Toleman team in Formula 1. He became F1 world champion three times, 1988, 1990, and 1991.

Below: Selena Quintanilla (1971–95) was shot in the back on April 31, 1995 by Yolander Saldivar, the founder of her first fan club and manager of Selena Etc,. in Corpus Christi, Texas. Selena had been singing since the age of eight and became a star in Tejano music with the band Selena y Los Dinos. By the late 1980s she was dubbed "la Reina de la Onda Tejana" (the Queen of Tejano music) but it wasn't until about 1993 that she came to more mainstream attention as she started singing more in English. Ironically, it took her death for more people to listen to her singing. Following her murder there was extra controversy over the new Texas concealed-handgun bill.

Right: John F. Kennedy Jr. was the son of president John F. Kennedy and Jacqueline Kennedy Onassis and many Democrats hoped that he would follow his father's footsteps into politics. He had been hinting that he was considering such a change of direction at the time of his death. John F. Kennedy Jr. studied law and worked for a few years in the Manhattan District Attorney's office before becoming founder and publisher of the political magazine *George*. As America's most eligible bachelor, his love life was minutely followed until he married Carolyn Bessette in 1996. Kennedy, his wife, and her sister were all killed when a private plane piloted by him disappeared into fog and crashed into the Atlantic Ocean near Martha's Vineyard on July 16, 1999.

Left: Diana, Princess of Wales, led a high-profile life in the public eye. Her every move was avidly followed by her many admirers. For this reason she gave her time and support to many good causes knowing the attention this would bring. Her particular interests were with children's charities, the ballet, AIDS, and the outlawing of land mines. Much of her effort was criticized as self-serving but it wasn't until her tragic death that the full extent of her work became known to the public.

Left: Known for his elegant outfits as much as for his fluid, stylish swing, Payne Stewart was playing some of his best golf at the time of his death. He enjoyed the limelight and his outlandish plus-fours and tam o'shanter made him unmistakable on the course. He is seen here reacting after sinking a birdie putt to capture the 71st PGA Championship at Kemper Lakes Golf course,. Hawthorn Woods, Illinois. On October 25, 1999, Stewart's life was tragically cut short in a private plane crash near Aberdeen, South Dakota while he was on his way to Texas.

Right: Coffin holding the body of R'n'B singer Aaliyah (born Aaliyah Dana Haughton) being carried from St. Ignatius Loyola Church following her funeral service in New York, August 31, 2001. Aaliyah died in a small Cessna 402 that crashed soon after take off from Marsh Harbour, in the Bahamas, on August 25. Six people died instantly, three others later. The 22-year-old Brooklyn-born New Yorker had traveled to the Bahamas to film her latest music video. Aaliyah was signed to the Blackground Enterprises label at the tender age of 13 and became a very successful recording artist. By the time she died she had made two successful films and was signed to make more, showing that she was much more than just a cross-over singer/actress.

1901–11
Career of Ulrich Salchow who wins most World and Olympic male figure skating titles (11).

1903
First Tour de France won by Maurice Garin.

1911
Clarence H. DeMarr wins first of seven Boston marathons (most).

1920
William Tilden wins first of seven US Men's Tennis Championships.

1927
Babe Ruth hits 60 home runs in a season for the Yankees.

1927–28
Dixie Dean scored top number of goals in a British Football Division 1 season (60).

1927–36
Career of Sonje Henie, most World and Olympic figure skating titles female (13).

1928–48
Test match career of Don Bradman (top test batting average ever).

1930
Uruguay wins first soccer world cup.

1936
Berlin Olympics—Jesse Owens wins four golds.
Ty Cobb first to enter NBA Hall of Fame as the player with most runs in a baseball career.

1936–63
Career of Archie Moore (129 KOs in a boxing career).

1941
Eddie Arcaro wins US Triple Crown on Whirlaway.
Margaret du Pont wins first of 25 titles in US tennis championships.

1947
Jackie Robinson becomes the first black baseball player in the major leagues.

1948
Eddie Arcaro wins second US Triple Crown (on Citation). London Olympics.

1949
First win by Bill Shoemaker (US jockey).

1954
Roger Bannister breaks 4min mile.

1956
Alfred Oerter wins first of four consecutive Olympic golds (US discus).
Jim Laker takes 19 wickets in a test match (v Australia).
Larissa Latynina wins first of 18 Olympic medals (most decorated female athlete).

1958–92
Career of Richard Petty (most Winston Cup wins—US NASCAR racing).

1959
Pele scores 126 goals in the season (in his career he will score 1,279 in 1,363 games from 1956-77).

1960
Paul Hornung scores 176 in an NFL season (record).

1960–81
A. J. Foyt Jr. most career car victories (67).

1960–61
Wilt Chamberlain averages 50.4 points in an NBA season.

1964
Cassius Clay defeats Sonny Liston.
Sam Snead (most career wins on US tour) wins his final US tour win at age 52 and 10 months.

1966
England wins soccer World Cup by beating W. Germany 4–2.

1966–75
Career of Giacomo Agostini (most world titles in motorcycle racing)

1968
Mexico Olympics includes Beamon's long jump record.
Arthur Ashe—first black to win US Open.

1969
Eddy Merckx wins his first Tour de France.
Rod Laver becomes first man to win tennis grand slam twice.

The twentieth century saw the expansion of sports into a worldwide industry commanding huge amounts of prime television time, providing massive numbers of people with employment, and generating huge profits for players and owners—a far cry from the amateur beginnings at the start of the century. Most of the games we play today were organized first in the nineteenth century. They were invented or codified, given common rules so that they could be played all over the world. They traveled with the great colonial powers or into their spheres of influence—so the British Empire played cricket and rugby, and Australia, the West Indies, India, and Pakistan still do today. Those areas under the United States' influence—particularly the Pacific Rim, play baseball and gridiron football.

Of all the sports and sporting events around the globe, two stand out: the Olympics, held every four years (except during WWI and WWII) and the football world cup. The modern Olympics originated in the mind of French educator Pierre de Fredi, Baron de Coubertin (1863–1937) who set up the first summer games in Athens in 1896. Even before radio and television existed to allow people to listen or watch the events around the globe they were successful, and a winter version was started in 1924. Unfortunately, the Olympic spirit has become tarnished in recent years: politics (terrorism in Munich in 1972, boycotts at Moscow in 1980 and Los Angeles in 1984), over commercialism, drugs, and the venality of the olympic hierarchy, all have contributed to a feeling that the games have got too big. Certainly the number of competitors has risen dramatically—Athens saw 311; Atlanta (1996) 10,310. It seems unlikely that they will survive in their current form, and most people would embrace a return to the basics of the Olympic motto—*Citius, Altius, Fortius* (Latin for Faster, Higher, Braver now translated as Swifter, Higher, Stronger.)

SPORTS

After the Olympics the FIFA World Cup is the biggest world event—and a true world event that attracts teams from countries all over the globe. Everyone plays soccer, men and women, and the four-yearly tournaments attract huge crowds and viewers, the latter larger than other sporting events such as the Olympics—3,587,583 spectators went to matches in 1994 when the U.S. hosted the cup; for France '98 there were 33.4 billion television viewers; payments for the television rights to the 2006 World Cup due to be held in Germany are going to be in excess of 1.5 billion Swiss Francs.

The World Cup was the idea of Frenchman Jules Rimet, whose name was given to the gold trophy awarded to the winning side. (Stolen in 1983, a new trophy was designed.) The first was held in 1930 in Uruguay. The hosts beat Argentina 4–2 in front of 93,000

spectators. Since then South American teams have dominated the cup, Brazil winning five times and Argentina twice. The women's event started in 1991 and has been won on two out of three occasions by the United States.

The world of sport may be dominated by big events, big money, and big TV companies, but there is no doubt that rich or poor, the peoples of the world love hitting, kicking, pushing, or propelling in some manner balls of all shapes and sizes into apertures, across lines, in water, on land; they love running and jumping, playing sports individually or as teams—and above all, they enjoy watching other people do it. Supporting your team at every level allows a cathartic experience, win or lose, and provides a common bond or common emnity to people from all walks of life. Some of the most important shared experiences, the most significant defining moments of the last century happened in stadiums, on sports fields, at golf courses the world over, as the photos in this chapter show.

1970
Gary Muhrcke wins first New York marathon. .

1971
Beth Bonner first women's New York marathon winner.
Billy Jean King makes over $100,000 in a season (first female athlete to do so.)

1971–79
Career of Annemarie Moser-Proll most alpine skiing world cup titles female (16).

1972
Munich Olympics is marred by Palestinian terrorism.
Mark Spitz wins seven golds in the pool.
Nikolay Andrianov wins first of 15 Olympic medals (most decorated male athlete)

1973
Secretariat wins the Kentucky Derby at a record speed

1975
First cricket world cup won by West Indies.

1976–84
Career of Ingemar Stenmark most alpine skiing world cup titles male (18).

1977
Red Rum Wins Third Grand National

1978
First Wimbledon title of Martina Navratilova (with 167 most tournament wins female ever).

1979
First race of Dale Earnhardt (top NASCAR moneywinner).

1988
Bjorn Borg wins fifth Wimbledon title.
Jack Nicklaus wins US Open with lowest total.

1981
First London marathon won in a dead heat by Inge Simonsen and Dick Beardsley (men).

1981–82
Wayne Gretzky scores 92 goals (most in NHL season).

1983
Serge Bubka wins his first World Championship pole-vaulting title. He will go on to set 35 world records.

1984
Carl Lewis wins first of four consecutive golds in long jump at Los Angeles Olympics.
Dan Marino gains 5,084 yards in a season NFL record (also most passing yards in NFL career).

1985
Pete Rose beats Ty Cobb's 57-year record for base hits.

1986
Michael Jordan scores 63 points in a game.

1987
New Zealand wins first Rugby world cup beating France.

1988
Ben Johnson disqualified in 100m Olympic sprint
Ivan Lendl plays in ninth consecutive ATP tour finals.

1989
Chris Evert retires (18 Grand Slam singles titles).
Kareem Abdul-Jabbar retires (top NBA point scorer and games played)

1992
Man Utd win first UK Premier Division title.

1993
Greg Norman—lowest total at British Open (267).
Retirement of Nolan Ryan (most career strikeouts in baseball/fastest pitcher of all time).

1994
Brian Lara scores 501* highest ever 1st class score.

1995
Don Shula retires (most successful NFL coach).
Philippe Sella plays last of 111 Rugby internationals.

1997
Robert Parish (most games, 1,611, in NBA/ABA) retires.
Tiger Woods—lowest winning score at US Masters (270) and youngest winner.

1999
Laffit Pincay Jr. passes Bill Shoemaker's win record.
Lance Armstrong wins his first Tour de France.

2000
Courtney Walsh becomes top test wicket taker (519).

Left: Babe Ruth was a giant of a player, the best striker of a ball in the game—as his 60 home runs in 1927 attest. It would take until 1980 before that record was beaten. Here he is in characteristic pose on October 14, 1924.

Below: Picture dated 1925 of Miss Gertrude Ederle & Helmy before they attempted to swim the Channel. Miss Ederle would become the first woman to do so in a time of 14hr 31min, two hours faster than the men's record at that time.

Left: This late 1930s photograph from the Baseball Hall of Fame Library shows New York Yankees' legend Joe DiMaggio (L) in action during a game with the Cleveland Indians. A three-time American League Most Valuable Player and lifetime .325 hitter, DiMaggio is also remembered for being Marilyn Monroe's second husband.

Above: The Third Test Match at Leeds. Don Bradman (left) and Stan McCabe of Australia going out to bat, July 12, 1930. "The Don" was the greatest batsman of his generation, possibly of all time. His career test batting average of 99.94 is unlikely to be beaten.

Above: On May 6, 1954, the impossible happened. Roger Bannister ran the mile in under four minutes—a record few had thought possible. A 25-year-old medical student, the photograph shows Bannister hitting the tape at an athletics meeting at Oxford.

Below: Mohammad Ali and Henry Cooper during their fight for the world heavyweight title—retained by Mohammed Ali—at Arsenal Stadium, Highbury, London. Cooper fans will remember Ali's knockdown and the bell that saved him in the third.

Above: Joy for Bobby Moore (center), Nobby Styles (right) and Manager Alf Ramsey (in blue) as the hold the Jules Rimet trophy on July 30, 1966. The final, against the then West Germany, was not without controversy. To this day there is argument about the eyesight of the touch judge who allowed the third goal.

Above: Mrs. Billie Jean King, the defending champion, in play against Miss I A R F Lofdahl of Sweden in the opening women's match on the Centre Court at Wimbledon, June 27, 1967. Mrs. King won 20 Wimbledon titles (then a record) between 1964 and 1979.

Left: Australia's Rod Laver shown during play on the Centre Court at Wimbledon, June 22, 1970. The first winner of two grand slams, many regard Laver as the greatest player of all time.

SPORTS

Left: August 31, 1972, and Mark Spitz notches up another gold at the Olympic Games in Munich. He won seven in total and while this feat has been equalled, no one who saw him in action would doubt that he was one of the greatest swimmers—if not the greatest—to have swum.

Below: Olga Korbut took the world by storm at the Montreal Olympics in 1976. Elfin grace and supreme athleticism made the Russian gymnast the darling of every crowd. Here she competes in the women's ninth European gymnastic championship, October 26, 1973.

Left: Garfield Sobers, now Sir Garfield, hits a four off England captain Tony Greig in the Lord's test of 1973. A brilliant player and great sportsman, Sobers will probably be best remembered for being the man who first hit six sixes in a six ball over (off the unlucky Glamorgan bowler Malcolm Nash).

Above: Jimmy Connors, here at 21 having won the men's singles championship at Wimbledon, proudly displays the Cup, while the Duke of Kent joins in the enthusiastic applause.

Below: Red Rum wins the Grand National for a record third time on April 3, 1977. The crowd goes wild as Red Rum, ridden by Tommy Stack, romps home at Aintree to make National Hunt history as winner of the Grand National Steeplechase for a record third time.

Above: As all the newspapers said, a "Love Match"—Jimmy Connors and his fiancée Chris Evert won the men's and women's singles at Wimbledon in 1974 and are seen with their trophies.

Above: Probably the best woman tennis player of all time, Czechoslovakia's Martina Navratilova is shown beating Chris Evert in the singles final on at Wimbledon on July 7, 1978. Navratilova would still be playing and winning titles in 2003.

Left: Jack Nicklaus and caddie "Tip" Anderson (left) make a study of the situation on the Old Course at St Andrews during a practice outing in preparation for the British Open golf championship, July 11, 1978.

Below: Sweden's Bjorn Borg drops to his knees while acknowledging the applause of tennis fans on Wimbledon's centre court after beating America's Roscoe Tanner to become the men's singles champion for an historic fourth successive year in 1979. He would win again next year as well.

Left: Bjorn Borg raises the Wimbledon men's singles trophy in triumph after winning the title for the third successive year, equaling the record set by Fred Perry in the 1930s. Borg beat American Jimmy Connors 6-2 6-2 6-3 in the final and would go on two win five finals in succession. He lost in the sixth final to John McEnroe. Borg retired in 1983 but returned to pro tennis twice unsuccessfully before taking part in the senior's (over 35s).

Above: Possibly the greatest of all time—American jockey Willie Shoemaker, seen on April 11, 1982, when 51 years old captaining the American jockeys for the third time in the USA v UK jockeys Challenge at Sandown Park. In a career spanning 33 seasons, Shoemaker rode over 8,100 winners.

Left: A 1980 photograph of the great Ingemar Stenmark, the Swedish alpine skiing star, showing off the two gold medals he won at the Winter Olympics in Lake Placid, US. He won the giant slalom and slalom events. Ski legend Stenmark was chosen as Sweden's sporting personality of the century, in a poll published on Friday, December 31, 1999.

Right: A 1987 photograph of French rugby star Philippe Sella, who played on the wing or at center for his national side a record 111 times in a career that spanned the period 1982–95. He retired from international rugby after the 1995 world cup, going on to play for English club Saracens. Sella had represented his country at a number of junior levels before receiving his first cap at age 20.

Below: Tiger Woods celebrates on the eighteenth green after winning the 1997 Masters tournament at Augusta National Golf Club in Georgia. Woods finished with a record 18-under-par. The most remarkable golfer of his generation, Tiger (real name Eldrick) was the first man to win the US junior amateur and amateur titles. He turned professional in 1996.

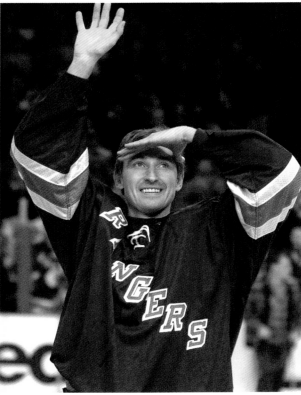

Above: Wayne Gretzky, the best ice hockey player ever, shields his eyes from the lights as he waves goodbye to fans at Madison Square Garden at his final game, April 19, 1999, against the Pittsburgh Penguins in New York, NY. Gretzky recorded an assist as the Rangers lost to the Penguins 2-1 in overtime.

Left: Kenny Brack (L) of Sweden waves to the crowd from the winners' circle as car owner and four-time Indianapolis 500 winner A.J. Foyt (R) drinks from the traditional jug of milk Sunday, May 30, 1999, after Brack won the 83rd running of the Indianapolis 500 at Indianapolis Motor Speedway in Indianapolis, Indiana. Foyt was born in Houston, Texas, and had a glittering racing career during which he became the first man to win the Indy 500 four times. He also won the Le Mans 24-hour endurance race and seven national championships before retiring in 1993.

Above: An October 1971 photograph of Wilt Chamberlain in action as a Los Angeles Lakers player. He was found dead at home on October 12, 1999, his death due to natural causes—he was 63 and had a history of heart problems. Ex-Globetrotter "Wilt the Stilt" will be remembered for being the NBA's MVP four times.

Above: One of the most famous men of the last 50 years: New Zealand legend and conqueror of Mt. Everest, Sir Edmund Hilary, gives the official address at the opening of the Louis Vuitton Challenge for the America's Cup to a crowd of thousands at the Auckland Viaduct Basin, on October 15, 1999. The America's Cup, after being in American possession from the 19th century until 1983, spent two short periods "Down Under" in the hands of first the Australians—who did what no one else had been able to do for 132 years and beat the American team in 1983—and then the New Zealanders who won in 1993. Today the cup resides in Switzerland, having been won in 2003 in a Switzerland–New Zealand final.

SPORTS

Left: Jockey Laffit Pincay Jr., of Panama takes win number 8,832 of his career, riding Millie's Quest, on December 8, 1999, at Hollywood Park Racetrack in Inglewood, California. The win, which came in the day's sixth race on the turf track, put him just one shy of the record of 8,833 career wins held by Bill Shoemaker. Pincay would go on to surpass Shoemaker's record later in the same month. He would retire with 9,530 wins in 2003.

Below: Dale Earnhardt (L) gets slammed by Ken Schrader (R) on turn four of the final lap of the Daytona 500 at Daytona International Speedway February 18, 2001, in Daytona Beach, FL. Earnhardt, 49, one of the greatest stars in auto racing history, died from injuries sustained in the crash.

Left: England's starting eleven for the Nationwide Friendly International at Pride Park, Derby between England and Mexico, May 25, 2001. Back row: (left to right) Ashley Cole, Emile Heskey, Martin Keown, Rio Ferdinand, Nigel Martyn and Phil Neville. Front row (from left) Michael Owen, Paul Scholes, Robbie Fowler, David Beckham (captain) and Steven Gerrard.

Below: This photograph, dated January 12, 2002, shows guard Michael Jordan (C) dunking for two of his first-half 26 points, against Minnesota Timberwolves center Leon Woods (L) at the MCI Center in Washington DC. Born in Brooklyn in 1963, Jordan, the greatest all-round basketball player ever, has set numerous records mainly playing for the Chicago Bulls. He also won Olympic gold with the US basketball team in 1984 and 1992.

Left: St. Louis Cardinals' Mark McGwire hits his 19th home run of the season in the sixth inning against the Atlanta Braves', August 1, 2001. The home run sets a Major League record: nine straight home runs in nine consecutive hits. It also ties him on the all time home run list with Harmon Killebrew at 573 career home runs. McGwire will be best remembered for the home run chase of 1998 when he and Sammy Sosa hit 70 and 66 respectively.

SPORTS

Left: Brian Lara of the West Indies celebrates scoring a century in the opening game of the 2003 Cricket World Cup at Newlands stadium in Cape Town, South Africa, February 9, 2003. A brilliant attacking batsman Lara is the holder of many individual batting records including the all-time highest test score of 375.

Below: The Williams sisters are the best women tennis players in the world, as the 2003 Wimbledon championship proved. Serena Williams (left) looks at her sister Venus after winning the ladies final at the All England Lawn Tennis Championships at Wimbledon on July 5.

Above: Michael Schumacher pushes his Ferrari through Club Corner on his way to victory in the Foster's British Grand Prix at Silverstone, Northamptonshire. on July 7, 2002. Comprehensively dominating recent Formula One history, Schumacher's Italian team won three consecutive drivers' championships 1999–2002.

Michael Schumacher was born in Hürth-Hermuhlheim in 1969. The outstanding driver of recent years, he won the Formula 1 World Championship in 1994 and 1995 with Benetton before moving to Ferrari in 1996 with a $26 million contract. Lean years 1996–98 made people wonder whether he had made a sensible choice: the

last three seasons have showed he was right. Schumacher learned his craft gokarting from the age of 4. The speed genes obviously run in the family: his brother Ralf has shown himself to be an excellent F1 driver.

I n the twentieth century entertainment changed from the intimate and personal small-scale "in the flesh" vaudeville audiences to multimillions entertained globally via radio, film, satellite, and television. Through the electronic media people have become accustomed and familiar with cities and environments from the other side of the world. Entertainers, who in former times would only be known to a live audience that came to see them, are now familiar faces around the world. Entertainment has become a billion dollar industry in which many fortunes have been made and lost.

At the turn of the century entertainment for most people meant traveling players, circuses, fairs, and vaudeville. A few were lucky enough to live near a nickelodeon that was showing the very latest technology—moving pictures. Money started to roll in and

shrewd businessmen spotted the potential of movies. The technology rapidly improved and by 1914 Hollywood had already set up as the hub of the movie industry and the star system had been devised. Millions flocked to see the movies and were enthralled by the stars.

In 1925 Ben Hur became the most expensive silent film ever, costing $3.9 million, a staggering amount of money at the time. The Academy of Motion Picture Arts and Sciences was founded May 4, 1927, and announced it would give "awards for merit or distinction." By 1931 the statuettes the Academy awarded were popularly known as the Oscars.

Talking pictures arrived in 1927 and an entire new generation of actors dominated the screen. Now movies came with their own sound effects and background music as well as dialogue. The technology for color films appeared in the 1930s but was not widely used in the movies until the late 1950s.

ENTERTAINMENT

Alongside the growth of the movies was the explosion of radio. Radio broadcasting became routine by the 1920s when institutions like the British Broadcasting Company came into being. This medium came directly to the audience in their homes and was used for education as well as entertainment. The first soap operas—so called because the sponsors of the serials were often soap manufacturers—enthralled audiences and their characters exploits were eagerly followed. Radio was king for about forty years until the first flickering images appeared on television. This required expensive technology to view, but nevertheless TV sets were eagerly bought by a public delighted to enjoy variety shows and soap operas in the comfort of their own homes.

Parallel to the movies the music industry developed, creating its own stars and accompanying publicity machines and hype. The hand-cranked gramophone gave way to the electric record player in the 1920s. Classical as well as popular music was widely enjoyed in the home and new disks were eagerly anticipated. The industry steadily grew with the Jazz Age in the 1930s and 1940s and then rock and roll in the 1950s and 1960s. Popular singers such as Frank Sinatra and Elvis Presley appeared in movies and on disk to satisfy the demands of their voracious fans.

In the early 1960s the Beatles appeared and record sales hit all time highs. They became global stars and arguably the most recognizable people on the planet. Since then many individuals and groups have found success and an accompanying millionaire lifestyle. By the end of the century the entertainment industry was worth billions of dollars and is confidently expected to grow even bigger and more powerful with its accompanying global marketing.

Vladimir Nabokov's scandalous novel of middle-age lust for "nymphet" Lolita.
Disneyland opens in California on July 18.

1957
Jack Kerouac On the Road published.
Beatnik movement originates in California. Perceived as dangerously bohemian.

1958
West Side Story, the musical by Leonard Bernstein.
First James Bond film, Dr. No starring Sean Connery.

1960
Films: A Man for all Seasons, La Dolche Vita, Psycho, Exodus.
Regular color TV transmission starts in Japan.

1961
Harper Lee wins Pulitzer Prize for To Kill a Mockingbird.
Rudolf Nureyev defects from Russia, claims asylum in Paris.

1962
David Lean's film Lawrence of Arabia stars Peter O'Toole.
Alexander Solzhenitsyn's One Day in the Life of Ivan Denisovich published.

1963
Joseph L. Mankiewicz's extravagant film Cleopatra, starring Elizabeth Taylor and Richard Burton.

1964
With Peyton Place, televised soap operas move to prime time.
Beatles conquer America.
William Burroughs' seminal beat novel The Naked Lunch published.
Films: Mary Poppins, Lord of the Flies, A Hard Day's Night, Goldfinger, Dr. Strangelove.

1965
Pirate radio stations operate off shore Britain. Radio Caroline the most successful.
Sound of Music phenomenally popular film.

1966
Star Trek lands on TV.
New York Herald Tribune stops publishing.
Frank Sinatra has international hit with My Way.
Public Broadcasting Service, PBS, is created.
The Woodstock music festival.

1970
Butch Cassidy and the Sundance Kid makes superstars of Robert Redford and Paul Newman.

1971
Stanley Kubrick's Clockwork Orange.

1972
HBO starts pay-TV service for cable.
The Godfather, first film of Mafia family trilogy.

1973
Films: The Exorcist, Last Tango in Paris, American Graffiti.

1974
Carrie is the first of Stephen King's blockbuster horror novels.
Punk rock music erupts in Britain, with themes of nihilism, anarchy.

1975
TV miniseries, Roots draws 130 million viewers over 8 nights.
Disco music becomes the rage.
Star Wars opens, first of the modern blockbusters.

1980
CNN, 24-hour news channel, begins reports.

1981
750 million watch wedding of Charles and Diana, July 29.

1985
Live Aid concert raises money for Third World poverty and revives many old rockers' careers.

1995
Toy Story is the first totally digital feature-length film

1997
Blockbuster Titanic released Takes box office by storm.

1998
Harry Potter and the Sorcerer's Stone, the first of the bestselling J.K. Rowling series published.

2001
Films: Lord of the Rings 1, Shrek, Harry Potter 1, Crouching Tiger, Hidden Dragon.

2002
Star Wars: Attack of the Clones first big budget film shot with digital cameras.

Left: Escapologist Harry Houdini in a photograph dated 1911. Born in Budapest as Erich Weiss, Houdini started as a trapeze artist before becoming the world's most famous escapologist. He died in 1926 after having been punched in the stomach by someone who wanted to test his ability to take any punch. The injury he sustained led to peritonitis.

Right: Comedian Harold Lloyd is featured here with Mildred Davis in a publicity still for the 1921 film *A Sailor-Made Man.* Lloyd and Davis married in 1923 and remained husband and wife until her death in 1969. Born in Burchard, Nebraska, Harold Lloyd is remembered for his character—the shy boy with spectacles and a solemn face—and his stunt work. Brilliant in silent movies such as *Safety Last* and *Why Worry?*, his career stalled when talkies arrived.

Right: Charlie Chaplin's 1928 Academy Award-winning silent film *The Circus* stars Chaplin as a tramp who falls in love with a circus owner's acrobatic daughter. At the first Academy Awards presentation on May 16, 1929, Chaplin was awarded the special statuette for "versatility and genius" in acting, writing, directing and producing *The Circus*. Born in Kennington, London, in 1889, he went to Hollywood in 1914. On the back of a string of successful films he formed United Artists with Douglas Fairbanks, Snr, and D. W. Griffith. His left wing politics did not find favor with the McCarthyist America of the 1950s and he left the United States for Switzerland. He was knighted in 1975 two years before his death.

Left: One of the greatest movies of the century, *Gone with the Wind*—the only novel written by Margaret Mitchell— starred Clark Gable and Vivien Leigh as Rhett Butler and Scarlett O'Hara. Although both Gable and Leigh received Academy Award nominations for their portrayals, only Leigh took home the Oscar (for Lead Actress). Gable, who had won an Oscar in 1934 for his role in *It Happened One Night*, went on to serve in the US Air Force before returning to film making. Mitchell's love story, set against a Civil War background, took her ten years to write. It won her the Pulitzer Prize and sold over 25 million copies.

Left: The 1941 Academy Award-winning film *How Green Was My Valley* starred Walter Pidgeon as the village preacher Mr. Gruffydd and Roddy McDowall as Huw Morgan. The film was nominated for 10 Academy Awards and won five including Best Picture. John Ford's film is a masterpiece of human drama. Adapted from Richard Llewellyn's bestselling novel, it tells the story of a Welsh coal-mining family at the turn of the 20th century.

Below: A scene still from the 1942 wartime drama *Mrs. Miniver*, which won the Oscar for Best Picture, featured Henry Wilcoxon as the Vicar. The film received 12 Academy Award nominations and won six statuettes, including William Wyler's first Oscar as Best Director. He would win two more, in 1946 for *The Best Years of Our Lives*, and in 1959 for the epic *Ben Hur*.

Right: Humphrey Bogart and Ingrid Bergman starred in *Casablanca*, the classic Oscar-winning film of 1943. Bogart was nominated for an Academy Award in the Lead Actor category for his portrayal of Café Americain owner Rick Blaine. In total, *Casablanca* received eight Oscar nominations and won three, including Best Picture. Bogart, born in New York City in 1899, won a Best Actor Oscar for his role in *The African Queen* opposite Katharine Hepburn. Married to Lauren Bacall, he died in 1957. Bergman won Academy awards for Best Actress in 1944 for *Gaslight* and 1956 for *Anastasia*, and as Best Supporting Actress in *Murder on the Orient Express* in 1974.

Above: A scene still from the 1944 film *Going My Way* features (left to right) Bing Crosby, Gene Lockhart, and Barry Fitzgerald. Oscar history was made when Fitzgerald became the first and only actor to be nominated in both the Lead Actor and Supporting Actor categories for the same performance. This is no longer possible. Fitzgerald won the Supporting Actor Oscar while his costar Crosby won the Oscar for Lead Actor. Born Harry Lillis Crosby in Tacoma, Washington, in 1904, his film career is best remembered for the "Road to . . ." movies with Bob Hope and Dorothy Lamour.

Above: A scene from the Academy Award-winning film *Hamlet* featuring Laurence Olivier as Hamlet and Eileen Herlie as Gertrude, the Queen. Olivier won the Lead Actor Oscar for his portrayal of the Prince of Denmark in the 1948 film. Made a life peer in 1970, in later years he is remembered for his role in the TV production of *Brideshead Revisited*.

Left: A publicity still from the 1950 Academy Award-winning drama *All about Eve* featuring (left to right): Gary Merrill, Bette Davis, George Sanders, Anne Baxter, Hugh Marlowe, and Celeste Holm. *All about Eve* received a record 14 Academy Award nominations and won six Oscars, including Best Picture.

Above: The all-star circus extravaganza, *The Greatest Show on Earth* received five Academy Award nominations and won two, including Best Picture of 1952. Pictured left to right: Lane Chandler, Cornel Wilde, James Stewart, Betty Hutton, Charlton Heston, John Ridgely, and Gloria Grahame

Right: Bing Crosby waves a greeting as he arrives at Plymouth aboard the liner *Liberte* from New York, September 9, 1952.

Left: Burt Lancaster and Deborah Kerr, shown here in a famous scene still from the 1953 Academy Award-winning film *From Here to Eternity;* both received Oscar nominations for their roles in the film. Lancaster was nominated in the Best Actor category for his portrayal of Sgt. Milton Warden, while Kerr received a Best Actress nomination for her role of Karen Holmes. The film received 13 nominations in total and won eight Oscars including Best Picture. Lancaster would win an Oscar for Elmer Gantry (1960); Deborah Kerr a special Academy Award in 1994.

Below: The 1954 Academy Award-winning drama *On the Waterfront,* starred Marlon Brando (center) as ex-prize fighter Terry Malloy. Lee J. Cobb (left) and Rod Steiger (right) costarred as Johnny Friendly and Charlie Malloy respectively.

Left: Actors Tom Ewell (L) and Marilyn Monroe (R) in a scene from the 1955 film *The Seven Year Itch*, written and directed by Billy Wilder. Austrian-born Wilder died on March 27, 2002, of pneumonia at the age of 95 in his Beverly Hills home. During his long career he had earned a total of 21 Academy Award nominations and produced some classic films—including the remarkable *Some Like it Hot*, with Marilyn Monroe, Tony Curtis, and Jack Lemmon, one of the seven films he made with Lemmon. Born in Austria in 1906, he worked as a journalist in Berlin before emigrating to Hollywood in 1933 after the rise of Adolf Hitler. He became a US citizen in 1935.

Below: *The Bridge on the River Kwai* starred Alec Guinness (left), William Holden (center) and Jack Hawkins (right). It won seven Academy Awards including Best Picture. Guinness also won the Oscar for Best Actor for his portrayal of British soldier Colonel Nicholson.

Left: Jayne Mansfield, at the Carlton Theatre, Haymarket, London, where her new film *Oh! for a Man* was being premiered. The classic blonde bombshell, Vera Jayne Palmer was born on April 19, 1933, and had starred in a number of films before a car crash cut short her career at age 34.

Below: The 1959 drama *Ben Hur* won a record-breaking 11 Oscars at the 32nd Academy Awards. The film, which starred Charlton Heston in the title role, took top honors when it was named the Best Picture of the year. Until the advent of computer special effects it was, without doubt, the most amazing recreation of Ancient Rome seen on film. Today Heston (born 1923 as Charles Carter) is known for his work on behalf of the National Rifle Association, of which he was an effective President for an unprecedented three terms.

Left: American actress Jayne Mansfield in costume for a night club scene in the film *Too Hot To Handle*, filmed at MGM's Elstree Studios on September 15, 1959. A press release of November 28, 1998, outlined that she had taken second place in a list of the world's 100 sexiest women this century. The survey, published by the men's magazine *Playboy*, crowned sex symbol Marilyn Monroe as the "steamiest siren in the world."

Right: One of the great cause célèbre's of the 1960s, it's difficult to understand why D. H. Lawrence's slim novel created so much fuss. "Now YOU can read it," says the showcard on the parcels of orange and white paperbacked copies of *Lady Chatterley's Lover* which were being despatched by Penguin Books. An Old Bailey jury decided that Penguin was not guilty of publishing an obscene novel which meant that the novel could be published as D. H. Lawrence wrote it.

Above: Natalie Wood starred as Maria in the 1961 musical *West Side Story*. The film was nominated for 11 Oscars and won 10 at the 34th Academy Awards. Natalie Wood achieved cinema fame with her excellent work in *Rebel Without a Cause* (1955), for which she received a Best Supporting Actress nomination, and other starring roles in the 1960s. In 1981 she drowned after falling from her yacht.

Right: One of the great films and two great performances—Peter O'Toole and Omar Sharif are seen in the 1962 Academy Award-winning film *Lawrence of Arabia* directed by David (later Sir David) Lean. The film, which received 10 Oscar nominations including a Best Actor nod for O'Toole and a Best Supporting Actor nomination for Sharif, won seven including Best Picture.

ENTERTAINMENT

Left: Before its time! The caption to this 1962 Press Association photograph reads: "Diana Stones, 20, turns the key prior to selecting the desired channel on a TV set equipped with the new Marconi PayVision system in a London demonstration. The unit, a small box no larger than the average book, plugs into the aerial socket of any standard TV set and push-buttons select various PayVision channels. It costs only £5 [$7.50] to instal and average cost of programmes is 2/6d [$0.20], with some public service and educational prgrammes free of charge. A central billing exchange automatically registers all programmes viewed. PayVision uses a closed circuit distribution system to bring three new TV channels into the home. The unit can be used with existing sets and does not affect present programme reception."

Right: Audrey Hepburn and Rex Harrison starred in the 1964 Academy Award-winning film *My Fair Lady*. The film was nominated for 12 Academy Awards and won eight, including Best Picture. Harrison received the Best Actor Oscar for his portrayal of Professor Henry Higgins, who transforms Hepburn's character—Eliza Doolittle—from a flower seller into a lady. *My Fair Lady* was a brilliantly populist rendition of Shaw's play *Pygmalion* and Harrison's understated style made him the perfect actor for a range of other films, such as *Blithe Spirit* (1945) and *Dr. Doolittle* (1967).

Right: Honor Blackman (Pussy Galore) meets Sean Connery (James Bond) before the filming of the third Bond movie, *Goldfinger.* Connery wasn't the first choice for Bond, but he made the part his own in the first film (*Dr. No*), going on to star in a total of seven. Other roles included *Indiana Jones and the Last Crusade* (1989) and *The Hunt for Red October*, the 1990 film of Tom Clancy's bestselling submarine thriller. Honor Blackman's repertoire included TV work appearing opposite Patrick McGoohan in *The Avengers.*

Below: Home from their successful tour of America, the Beatles leave the plane at London Airport to a welcome from their fans, September 21, 1964. Left to right Ringo Starr, John Lennon, George Harrison, and Paul McCartney.

Left: Legendary US singer Frank Sinatra in a picture dated April 1968 at Orly airport arrives in Paris. Sinatra died of a heart attack on May 15, 1998, at the age of 82. An accomplished actor, it is as a popular singer of the late 1950s/early 1960s that many remember him, with songs such as "New York, New York" and "Come Fly With Me."

Left: *Midnight Cowboy* starred Jon Voight as Joe Buck and Dustin Hoffman as Ratso Rizzo. Both Voight and Hoffman were honored with Academy Award nominations in the Best Actor category for their performances in the film. *Midnight Cowboy* received seven Academy Award nominations and won three including Best Picture of 1969.

Left: Gene Hackman starred as New York City narcotics officer Jimmy "Popeye" Doyle in the 1971 film *The French Connection*. Hackman won the Best Actor Oscar for his performance in the film, which was named Best Picture at the 44th Academy Awards. Born in 1930 in San Bernadino, California, Hackman also won Academy Award nominations for *Bonnie and Clyde* (1967), I *Never Sang For My Father* (1970), and *Mississippi Burning* (1988), and a Best Supporting Actor Oscar for his part in *The Unforgiven* (1992).

Right: *The Godfather*—the first in a trilogy—starred Al Pacino (seated) as Michael Corleone and Marlon Brando as Don Vito Corleone. Pacino was nominated in the Best Supporting Actor category for his performance in the film. Although Brando won the Best Actor Oscar, he declined the award.

Left: Robert Redford (left) and Paul Newman (right) costarred in the Academy Award-winning film *The Sting*. Newman portrayed con artist Henry Gondorff while Redford played grifter Johnny Hooker. Redford was nominated for an Academy Award in the Best Actor category for his performance in the film. A brilliant pairing, Newman and Redford also made *Butch Cassidy and the Sundance Kid*.

Right: Ballet dancer turned actor Rudolf Nureyev in London before the Royal Premiere of his first film, Valentino on October 3, 1977.

Left: Rudolf Nureyev and members of the Zurich Ballet during rehearsals for *Manfres.*

Right: In the 1970s his father promoted him together with his brothers in the Jackson Five; In December 1982 he succeeded with his break-through album *Thriller.* There's no doubting his brilliance but Jackson's odd behavior has always sounded a note of caution on his career.

Above: A brilliant idea, brilliantly executed. Horrified and ashamed at the plight of Africa in general, and starving Ethiopia wrecked by civil war, Live Aid organizer Bob Geldof cajoled, threatened, and bullied the audience to provide funds for the Third World. Here he is seen on stage during the charity fund raising concert at Wembley, London.

Right: Billy Zane and Leonardo Dicaprio at the royal movie premiere of *Titanic* at the Odeon in Leicester Square, London, November 18, 1997. By 2001 it was the biggest movie of all time, having grossed $1,835,100,000 worldwide—with the next highest (Star Wars 1) on 922, 600, 000.

Above: Novelist Stephen King is one of the most successful horror story tellers ever and many of his books have been made into successful films. He had the urge to write even when he was a child but it took a while before he was successfully published. After receiving a number of rejections for his stories he submitted *Carrie* to Doubleday in 1973 and they accepted the manuscript for publication. Four months later the paperback rights sold for $400,000. King quit his day job (teaching) and took up writing full time. His books are now translated into 33 languages and sell in over 35 different countries making a staggering 300 million plus, copies.

Right: Stanley Kubrick, the maverick film director, was a New Yorker but lived in England as a recluse from 1961 until his death in March 1999. He directed a number of notable films including *Dr Strangelove* (1963), *2001; a Space Odyssey* (1968), *A Clockwork Orange* (1971), and *Eyes Wide Shut* (1997), his last film.

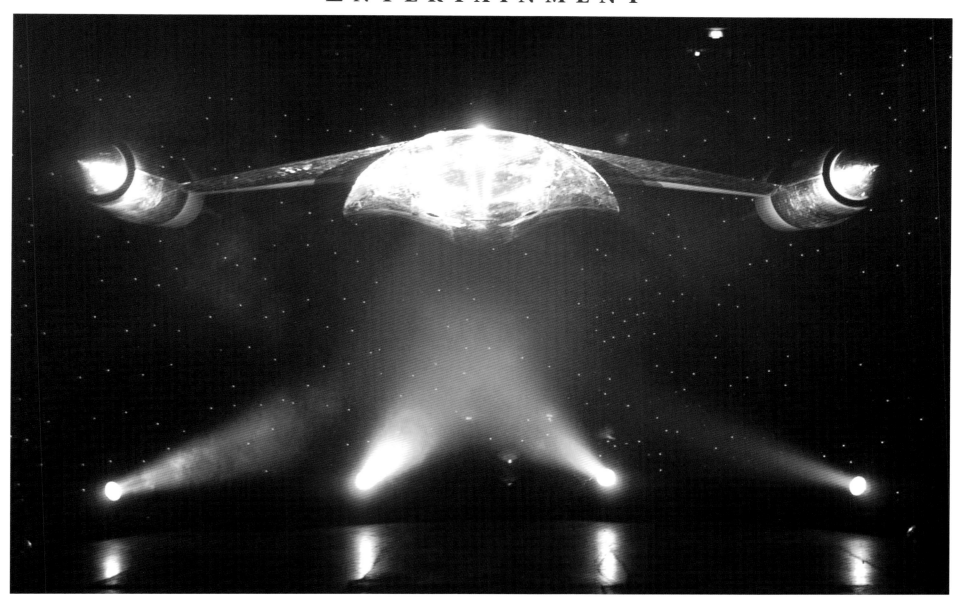

Above: A life size replica of a Naboo N-1 Starfighter, used in the making of *Star War 1, The Phantom Menace.* The model flies with the help of cables but in the film it carries lethal weapons—laser cannon and twin fire-linked Proton torpedoes. Its job is to protect the skies and space around the planet of Naboo. The two radial J-type engines are capped in gleaming chrome and trail long delicate-looking finials behind the ship's single-pilot compartment. Behind the pilot sits a standard astromech droid, plugged into the starfighter.

Right: The enormous and lucrative hand held video game market is dominated by Japanese products. Here visitors at the annual Tokyo Toy Show 2001 try out Nintendo's latest game console, the "GameBoy Advance." The product features a 32-bit RISK processor on its CPU and 32,000-color LCD display. It was put on sale on March 21, 2001, with a price tag of 9,800 yen ($80 US).

Left: The London Imax cinema at Waterloo, central London, is a 477-seat state-of-the-art large-format cinema. It was opened on August 16, 2001, and was made possible thanks to £15 million (around $22.5 million) from the Arts Council of England's Lottery Fund. The screen is over 20 meters high and 26 meters wide and the sound system is 11,600-watt digital surround-sound. The auditorium features 14 tiered rows of seats that enable all viewers—even children—to enjoy full, unobstructed views of the picture. The building that houses it is illuminated with colored lights at night and is designed by award-winning architect Bryan Avery of Avery Associates Architects.

Below: Two young Harry Potter fans dressed as their hero queue up outside the Odeon cinema at Leicester square in central London, November 16, 2001. Thousands flocked to the cinema for the first day of public showing of the much anticipated film based on J. K. Rowling's books. Cinema theaters across the country have recorded the largest amount of pre-bookings ever.

Above: One of the most eagerly anticipated films ever (and dreaded by avid fans) was *Lord of the Rings: The Fellowship of the Ring.* The world premier was held on December 10, 2001 at the Odeon Leicester Square, London and nobody was disappointed. Among the attending stars were Billy Boyd (right) who plays "Pippin," Elijah Wood who plays "Frodo," and Dominic Monaghan (left) who plays "Merry."

Right: Eager fans waiting for stars at the world premiere of the "Fellowship of the Rings," the first installment of the trilogy of books known collectively as *The Lord of the Rings.* The next two films are called *The Two Towers* and *The Return of the King.* The director Peter Jackson assembled a large ensemble cast and filmed for 18 months in his native New Zealand using the stunning landscape as the backdrop for this timeless epic.

Above: Awards time at the 74th Academy of Motion Picture Arts and Sciences, in Hollywood, California, March 24, 2002. Posing with Oscars for best Visual Effects for the movie *The Lord Of The Rings: The Fellowship Of The Ring* are (from left to right) Jim Rygiel, Randall William Cook, Richard Taylor, and Mark Stetson.

Right: Scottish actor Ewan McGregor, one of the stars of *Star Wars: Episode II Attack of the Clones*, poses for photographers and fans at the film's premiere with Darth Vader and Storm Troopers in Los Angeles, May 12, 2002. The event was one of eleven charity premieres held across the US and Canada. The 5 films in the Star Wars franchise have already grossed close to $4 Billion, and there's still one more film to come.

Above: Best Motion Picture of the Year, to nobody's very great surprise, was *Lord of the Rings: The Two Towers*.

Below: The 75th Anniversary Oscar Winner Reunion Photo.

Top Row: Julie Andrews, Kathy Bates, Halle Berry, Ernest Borgnine, Red Buttons, Nicolas Cage, Sir Michael Caine, George Chakiris, Jennifer Connelly, Sir Sean Connery, Geena Davis, Daniel Day-Lewis, Olivia de Havilland, Kirk Douglas, Michael Douglas, Robert Duvall, Louise Fletcher.

Second Row: Brenda Fricker, Cuba Gooding Jr., Louis Gossett Jr., Joel Grey, Tom Hanks, Marcia Gay Harden, Dustin Hoffman, Celeste Holm, Anjelica Huston, Claude Jarman Jr., Jennifer Jones, Shirley Jones, George Kennedy, Sir Ben Kingsley, Martin Landau, Cloris Leachman.

Third Row: Karl Malden, Marlee Matlin, Hayley Mills, Rita Moreno, Patricia Neal, Jack Nicholson, Margaret O'Brien, Tatum O'Neal, Jack Palance, Luise Rainer, Julia Roberts, Cliff Robertson, Mickey Rooney, Eva Marie Saint, Susan Sarandon.

Bottom Row: Maximilian Schell, Mira Sorvino, Sissy Spacek, Mary Steenburgen, Meryl Streep, Barbra Streisand, Hilary Swank, Jon Voight, Christopher Walken, Denzel Washington, Robin Williams, Teresa Wright.

Left stage: Adrien Brody.

Right: Chris Cooper, Nicole Kidman, Catherine Zeta-Jones, Peter O'Toole.

Above: The various Harry Potter books by J. K. Rowling are a genuine publishing sensation. Impatient fans had to contain themselves for three years for the fifth volume of the bestseller to appear on June 21, 2003. 13 million books were printed in the first edition for the worldwide sale. The latest book, called *Harry Potter and the Order of the Phoenix* was initially printed in English only, foreign language fans had to wait a few more months before getting their own version.